THE
BOGNOR BRANCH LINE

by
S. Jordan

THE OAKWOOD PRESS

ISBN 0 85361 393 1

Typesetting by Gem Publishing Company, Brightwell, Wallingford, Oxon

Printed by S & S Press, Radley, Oxfordshire.

A cartoon postcard commenting on the speed of the Bognor branch line train, c.1905.
Gerard Young Collection

Acknowledgements

Many people have helped in getting this book, (my first effort) into print. Among those I would like to thank are Roger Kidner who read the original manuscript and gave me many valuable suggestions, Claire Allwood who gave me free access to the Gerard Young Collection, Bertha Watson and my Father who shared their memories with me. I would also like to thank the staff's of the West Sussex Records Office, and the Bognor Regis and Chichester Central Libraries, without whose invaluable assistance this book would have been a pale shadow of its present form.

Published by
The OAKWOOD PRESS
P.O. Box 122, Headington, Oxford.

Contents

Members of the boys' brigade parade outside Bognor station on their way to annual camp at Pagham Harbour. *Author's Collection*

Bognor engine drivers pause for a photograph between drinks at the Lamb Inn, summer 1913.   *Author's Collection*

A Southdown motor company Charabanc, one of many which became serious rivals to the railway in the 1920s and 1930s.   *Author's Collection*

Chapter One
The Building of Bognor

"But what", said I, "shall I call Bognor? It is not a town, for it has no market: neither is it a village, having no parish church".

"Call it a place then", says Tim.

"That's a comprehensive term to be sure", replied I, "but how will it distinguish it from London, Chichester, Salisbury, etc?"

"A bathing-place, however you may call it".

"Well let it stand thus – Bognor a hamlet in the parish of South Bersted, a fashionable bathing-place in Sussex, seven miles from Chichester and about sixty-five from London; having commodious lodging-houses and famed for its alternately visible and invisible rocks". So said Timothy Type and Peregrine Project in their book on a walking tour of Sussex and Hampshire, published in 1802.

But how did this fashionable bathing-place come to be? To find the answer we must go back to 1784 when Sir Richard Hotham, a rich London hatter, came to stay at a small farmhouse near to the hamlet of Bognor on the Sussex coast. He had for sometime been unwell and friends recommended that he should get some sea air. His sojourn in Bognor revived him so much that he returned for the next two years for more of the same.

In December 1786 he purchased the farmhouse where he had stayed for £200 and set in motion plans to rebuild it as a home fit for a gentleman. At this time the Prince Regent was making both sea-bathing and Brighton popular with the well-to-do, and Hotham thought that if money could be made in Brighton then why not in Bognor? And so in 1788 when the rebuilding of his home was finished he set about putting his plans for a fashionable new bathing resort in motion.

He purchased a total of 180 acres of land for £6225 and built two rows of terraces, Hothampton Place and East Row. The following years saw the construction of many fine buildings, The Hotel, Chapel House, Dome House, a library and bath house, Spencer Terrace, and Hothampton Crescent. In 1791 when the construction work was completed the new town of Hothampton was opened for visitors.

The expected rush of well-to-do visitors did not, however, occur and Hotham made very little money for the first few years. There were a few notable patrons: the Duke of Devonshire, Lord Lucan, Lord Spencer, the Earl of Pembroke and in 1796 the Prince of Wales, but the place never became fashionable in the way that Hotham had envisaged and in 1799, on 13th March, he died. Loaded with debt his estates were sold piecemeal, raising £68,000 and leaving only £12,000 for his heirs after his debts were cleared. After his death the name Hothampton was quietly dropped.

During all this time the only access to Bognor was by road, Sussex lanes being notorious for having axle-breaking ruts in summer, and in winter for being a sea of mud. Any visitor from the capital had to endure a ten hour journey on the "Comet" post coach, which left the Ship Tavern at Charing Cross and arrived in Bognor at the New Inn, or travel by local carrier from Chichester or Brighton.

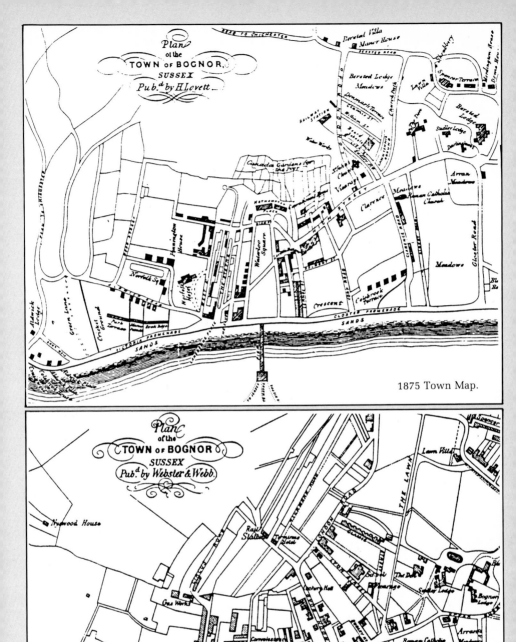

1875 Town Map.

1892 Town Map.

Since the first public meeting at the new Goodwood race course in 1802 Bognor had become a popular dormitory town for the better class of race-goers, and it was not long before Bognor landlords found that money could be made renting houses out for "Goodwood Week" at highly inflated rates.

The popularity of the town grew as word of its mild climate and pleasant situation spread, but, since the days of Hotham, very little building work had been done and now the problem was not how to attract visitors but where to put them when they came. An incentive to the builders of Bognor came in 1824, when the Surrey, Sussex and Hampshire Railway Company proposed a line from London to Portsmouth via Lewes, Brighton and Shoreham with lateral branches to "several maritime towns". Bognor was such a town and also being on the course of the railway it assumed that one of the "lateral branches" would find its way to the popular seaside resort.

Spurred on by the image of hundreds of rail-borne visitors, the Bognor New Town Company was formed in January 1825 with the purpose of transforming the many open spaces in and around the town into a maze of dwellings. The improvement company dragged its feet in the beginning, but after this slow start many fine new terraces were built. Unfortunately the railway did not come to the town, it was in fact not built at all, and not one inch of track laid. It would be a further forty years before the sound of a steam engine could be heard in the town.

In 1821 a future Queen of England came for a 3 month stay; Princess Victoria, then only three years old, stayed with Lord Arran who owned Bognor Lodge, Sir Richard Hotham's old farmhouse. She came back several times until 1830 and always had fond memories of her childhood days in the town, referring to it as "dear little Bognor".

The growth of the town continued during the 1830s but the majority of the visitors were well-off, what was needed was a means of bringing in hundreds, or even thousands, of short stay visitors into cheap lodging houses: so what was really needed was the introduction of the railway.

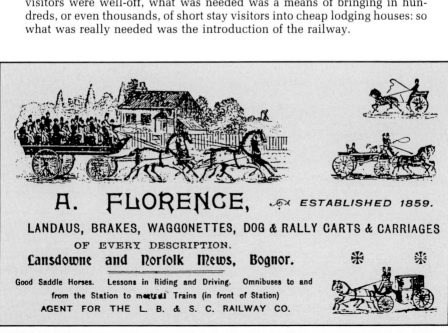

PROPOSED BOGNOR RAILWAY TERMINI
1845–1863

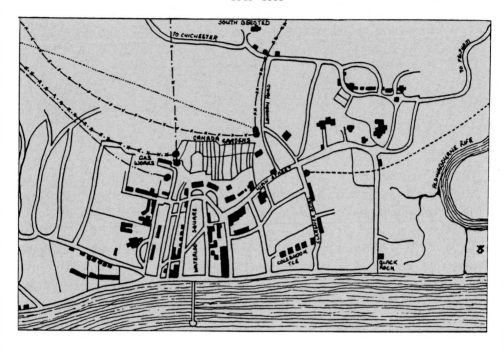

KEY

.... Chichester and Bognor Railway 1845

— — — — — — — — - Bognor Branch Railway 1845

—ı—ı —ı—ı—ı—ı Drayton and Bognor Railway 1846

— ·· — ·· — ·· — ·· Bognor Railway 1852

— · —×— —×— ·— Bognor Railway 1857/58

—×ı —×ı —×ı —×ı Bognor Railway 1860/61

—×·×—×·×—×·×·×· Bognor Chichester and Midhurst Railway 1860/1/2/3

Chapter Two
Plans and yet more Plans

1845 could have been Bognor's year for entering the Railway Age. Already railways were being introduced into the advertising for the town, notices claiming "London in 5½ hours" were placed in newspapers backed up by a description of the route to be taken by the intrepid traveller. To reach the Capital in the specified time the traveller needed to catch, at 8 o'clock in the morning, the *Railway Times* post coach (at the Norfolk Inn, Bognor) which proceeded to Shoreham and then to catch the London train from there. The return journey arrived back at the Norfolk Inn at 4.30 pm, thus requiring our traveller to stay overnight in the Capital.

Early in the same year the town commissioners proposed a plan for a canal and dock scheme. This was part of a larger scheme to join Portsmouth and London by means of an inland canal. This was supposed to enable naval and merchant shipping to travel between those two cities without having to use the sometimes dangerous English Channel. The English had long memories of the many wars with the French.

At the same time the London and South Western Railway sponsored a Bill through Parliament for a line to be built from Guildford via Chichester to Portsmouth, with a branch line from Chichester to Bognor. The plans, drawn up by Joseph Locke, had a proposed capital of £1m, later increased to £1¼m. Following a territorial agreement between the LSWR and the London and Brighton Railway, who were expanding their system westwards, the LSWR was precluded from the whole of Sussex. This meant that the line was only built as far as Godalming, 3½ miles to the south of Guildford.

In November a plan was put forward by one Edward Lomax for a line from Chichester to Bognor. This showed the line leaving a terminus to the north of London Road, and to the east of what is now Station Road, on the site now occupied by the Regal Bingo hall. The route followed an absolutely straight line north-north-east towards Chichester. After 3¾ miles it was to cross the Portsmouth–Arundel canal by means of a swivel bridge, passing through North Mundham and then to the north of the Chichester canal basin. The line then crossed the path of the as yet incomplete Chichester and Brighton Railway five miles and five furlongs from Bognor. The line carried on for a further 3¾ furlongs to a terminus next to the main Chichester–Portsmouth road. The total length of the line was 6 miles and 7 chains. Opposition from the London and Brighton Railway, which was to take over the Chichester –Brighton line on its completion, put paid to this scheme.

As a sop to the railway hopes of Bognor, the Brighton company put forward a scheme of its own for the town; its own "West Coast Line" had reached as far as Shoreham in 1840 and by 1845 it had progressed as far as Worthing and by June 1846 it would be open as far as Chichester. The South Bersted Vestry Committee received copies of the plan in December, and Mr Phillips, Surveyor of the Highways, issued a notice calling a Parish Meeting. It read:

PARISH OF SOUTH BERSTED

Notice is hereby given that a meeting will be held in the vestry room at the Parish Church on Friday next at 10 o'clock in the forenoon to take into considera-

Parish of South Bersted —

Notice is hereby given — That a Meeting will be held in the Vestry Room at the Parish Church on Friday next at ten o'clock in the Forenoon to take into consideration a notice served on the Surveyor of the Highways by the Solicitors of the Directors of the Brighton Railway, which Notice states that it is intended to form a Branch Railway to Bognor from and out of the Brighton and Chichester Railway, and that such Branch Railway will cross the Public Highway in the parish aforesaid leading from Bognor to Felpham and also another Public Highway maintained and repaired by the Parish afor.d called Gloucester Road, and the said Meeting will determine whether the Surveyor shall signify his consent thereto or not.

Parish

Notice of the meeting called by the South Bersted Vestry Committee.

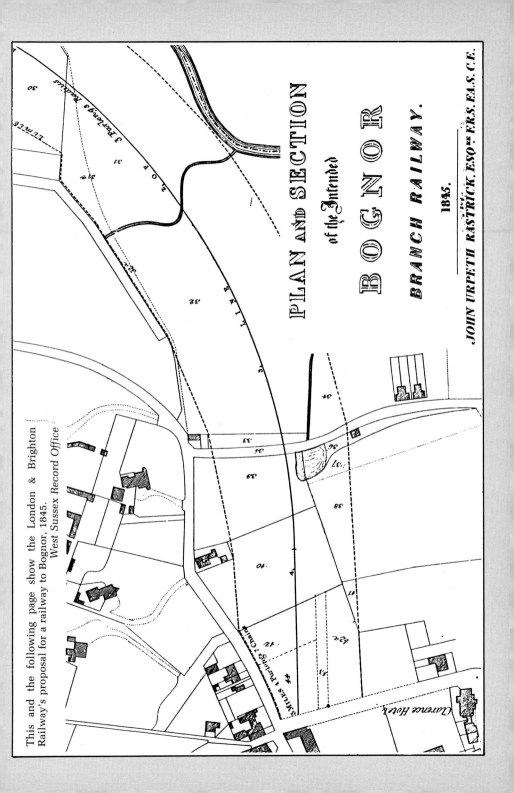

This and the following page show the London & Brighton Railway's proposal for a railway to Bognor, 1845. *West Sussex Record Office*

PLAN AND SECTION of the Intended BOGNOR BRANCH RAILWAY. 1845.

JOHN URPETH RASTRICK, ESQʳᵉ FRS. FAS. C.E.

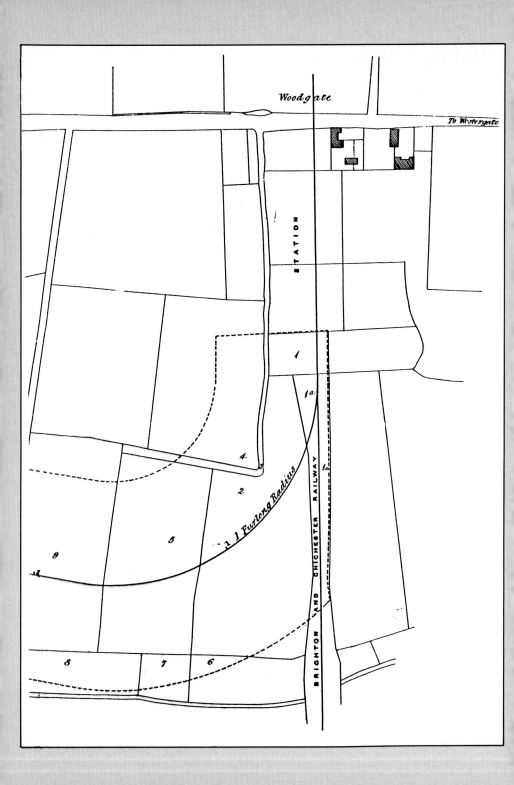

West Sussex Record Office

DRAYTON & BOGNOR RAILWAY

SUSSEX.

PLAN AND SECTION

1846.

HENRY & FREDK HITCHINS, ENGINEERS.

THOS WISDOM, SURVEYOR.

PLAN AND SECTIONS

OF THE

PROPOSED

BOGNOR RAILWAY.

1852.

J. NEVILLE WARREN, C.E.

The proposed Bognor Railway, 1852.   West Sussex Record Office

BOGNOR RAILWAY

SESSION 1857

H. H. BIRD, del.

THE PARK

(SELSEY BILL.)

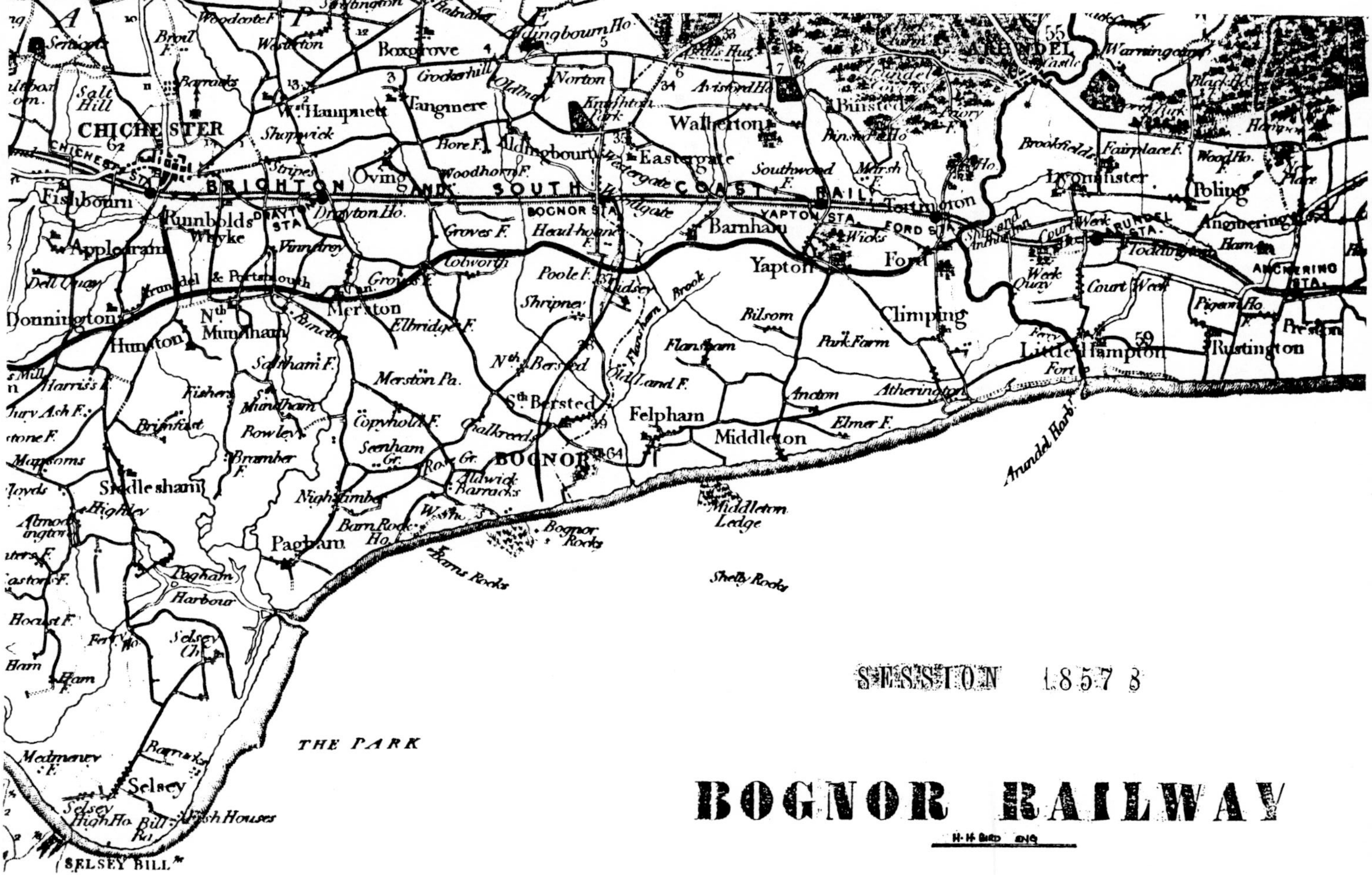

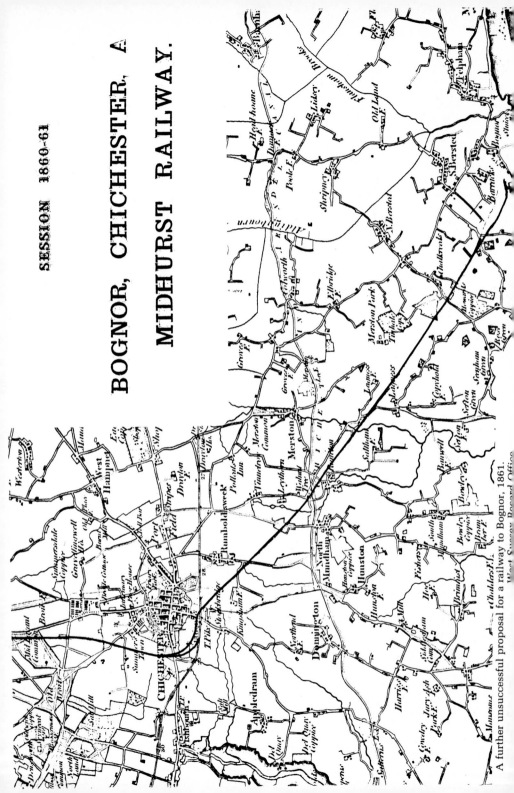

SESSION 1860-61

BOGNOR, CHICHESTER, A MIDHURST RAILWAY.

A further unsuccessful proposal for a railway to Bognor, 1861.
West Sussex Record Office

tion a Notice served on the Surveyor of Highways by the solicitors of the Directors of the Brighton Railway, which Notice states that it is intended to form a Branch Railway to Bognor from and out of the Brighton and Chichester Railway, and that such Branch Railway will cross the Public Highway in the Parish aforesaid leading from Bognor to Felpham, and also another Public Highway maintained and repaired by the Parish aforesaid called Gloucester Road, and the said meeting will determine whether the Surveyor shall signify his consent or not.

December 28th 1845

The plans, surveyed by J.U. Rastrick, showed the line leaving the Brighton–Chichester main line from the village of Woodgate, 3½ miles to the north of Bognor; it curved away in an east-south-east direction, then south in a 1 furlong radius curve for 2 furlongs, then heading south-south-east for 1 mile, 1 furlong and 2 chains. It passed Headhoane Farm at 5 furlongs and Oldlands Farm at 1 mile 7 furlongs 4 chains. The two major waterways on the route were the Portsmouth–Arundel canal, crossed at 6 furlongs by means of a bridge with a 25 ft span set at a height of 12 ft, giving a height above water of 15 ft, and the Aldingbourne Rife which was crossed at 2 miles, 2 furlongs and 4 chains and again at 2 miles 6 furlongs and 6 chains. After crossing Felpham Road and Gloucester Road the line arrived at a terminus in the open fields to the east of the Clarence Hotel and at the northern end of Clarence Road. Total length of the line was 3 miles 4 furlongs and 7 chains.

The estimated cost of the line was £38,000, excluding station buildings and Parliamentary costs. The scheme was only a half-hearted attempt by the Brighton Company, and also some unexpected help came from local landowners who did not want the line to pass through the low lying Brooklands, which would have been good building land needed when Bognor expanded further. Although Parliamentary approval was given in 1846, powers were allowed to lapse and no work was done on the line. The canal scheme mentioned earlier also failed because of railway opposition.

On 8th June, 1846 the Chichester and Brighton Railway opened its final section of track from Arundel and Littlehampton to Chichester. At its nearest point to Bognor, a little hamlet called Woodgate 3½ miles to the north of the town, the Chichester and Brighton Railway built a station called Bognor. As previously stated, at its opening the line was taken over by the London and Brighton Railway, now through amalgamation known as the London, Brighton and South Coast Railway. The station was built to the east of the point where the line crossed the main London–Bognor road, a level crossing and gate keeper's cottage being provided. In November 1846 the name was changed to Woodgate for Bognor, a more accurate description of its location, but then the following year the name reverted to that of Bognor. The first station master, Mr Robinson, stayed at the job for 16 years until his death in 1862 when he was succeeded by his daughter. Miss Robinson, who had been employed in the Booking Office, held the post for only one year until leaving in 1863 to get married. Swan's Omnibus met five of the daily trains to convey passengers to Bognor.

Having a station called Bognor, yet not actually in the town, was not enough for Bognor folk who wanted their own railway line into their own town station. So in 1846 a group of local business men put forward a scheme entitled the "Drayton and Bognor Railway". The plans were drawn up by Henry and Frederick Hitchins, Engineers, and Thomas Wisdom, Surveyor. The plan was for the branch to leave the main "West Coast Line" of the LB&SCR from a station to be built at the hamlet of Drayton, 2 miles east of Chichester and 3 miles north of Bognor. Heading east-south-east at a radius of 2 furlongs then south-east, the line crossed the Portsmouth–Arundel canal at North Mundham 1 mile and 3 furlongs from Drayton by means of a swivel bridge. The bridge had a span of 20 ft and was set to a height of only one foot above water level. The line continued almost dead straight for a further 3 miles and 7 furlongs to a terminus in the same place that Lomax chose for his Chichester–Bognor Railway of the previous year. The total length of the line was 4 miles and 2 furlongs. Even though local support was behind the plan, Parliamentary approval had already been given to the LB&SCR scheme, and the Drayton Railway did not get past the planning stage.

The mad rush of plans slowed down as the "Railway Mania" period passed into history, however the flow of ideas did not just stop dead, they merely regained their breath for a further attack. In 1852 another plan for a Bognor Railway was put forward by J. Neville Warren whose scheme had the branch line leaving the main line 1 furlong 4 chains to the east of Chichester station. Heading on a 1 furlong, 2 chain radius curve east-south-east towards Bognor, after 6 furlongs the line crossed the Portsmouth–Arundel canal at North Mundham by an opening arch bridge with a span of 14 ft. With the exception of a slight kink near the hamlet of Lagness, the line followed an almost straight route to the outskirts of Bognor, where at 5 miles 1 furlong the line took on a 4 furlong radius curve of very short duration. This brought the track on to the correct alignment to reach the terminus 5 miles 4 furlongs from the junction. The station was to have been south of the gas works on Ockley Road and west of Steyne Street. Again it was the same old story, lack of influential support and a shortage of cash killed the Bill in the Parliamentary stage.

The next person to get on the Bognor railway "merry-go-round" was Henry H. Bird, who was nothing if not persistent. This man produced no fewer than four different plans over a six year period. The first, published in 1857 and entered for Parliamentary consent in the 1857/8 Parliamentary session, showed the line leaving the existing Woodgate station from a facing junction in a south-easterly direction following a curve of 1 furlong, 2 chains radius until the 2 furlong point. The Portsmouth–Arundel canal was crossed just short of the 6 furlong point by means of an arched bridge with a span of 20 ft rising to 8 ft above water level. The track then followed a gentle double curve in to the Bognor terminus situated at the north end of Steyne Street and to the north-east of the gas works. This line like all the others failed at an early stage to win sufficient support and did not gain Parliamentary approval.

Chapter Three
The Line is Built

The year 1860 seemed to have brought with it a ray of light at the end of the tunnel; the Bognor Railway Company was formed by a group of local businessmen. Plans were laid before Parliamentary committee on 11th May, 1860 and with the backing of the London, Brighton and South Coast Railway, local landowners and townspeople the Bill was enacted as 24 and 25 Vic. Cap 120 on 11th July, 1861.

The Bognor Railway Company, whose offices were at 41 Parliament Street in London, had a working capital of £30,000 which was raised by the sale of 1500 shares at £20 each, the four Directors having to purchase 50 shares apiece. The Chief Executive of the company, Mr Joseph Cary, called a meeting of the Board at its London offices at which his fellow Directors, Mr William Edward Knobel, Mr Henry Hawes Fox, and Captain Robert O'Brian-Jameson entered into negotiations with the LB & SCR. Following these talks, the Brighton Company agreed to purchase the line when completed for £24,500, and further to erect a station building on land purchased by the Bognor Railway. The LB & SCR also agreed to provide the rails and sleepers for the permanent way.

Clause IX of the Act gave the Bognor Railway powers to enter into traffic agreements with the Brighton Company, who, as previously stated, were to take over the running of the line on its completion in any case.

Unlike the previous schemes for a line to Bognor this line was not to come from an existing station on the main line, it was however to have a brand new station built for its junction with the "West Coast Line". The new station was to be built near the small village of Barnham, between Ford and Woodgate stations, and was to be known as Barnham Junction.

Also in the running in the 1860/61 Parliamentary session was a private Bill to form the Bognor, Chichester and Midhurst Railway, again the Surveyor-Engineer was Henry H. Bird. This line was to have had its Bognor terminus in the open area known as Canada Gardens, and at right angles to Steyne Street. The route passed through the Parishes of South Bersted and Merston, crossed the Portsmouth and Arundel canal at North Mundham by an opening arch bridge with a 14 ft span and thence on through the Parish of Rumboldswhyke. Here the line merged with the Chichester–Brighton line until it passed Chichester station, then left the main line to head north through Lavant, West Dean and Cocking to Midhurst. The Chichester to Bognor section was 5 miles and 4 furlongs in length.

The Mayor of Chichester, Councillor Henty, was a shareholder and Director of the proposed line, and the *Chichester Journal* for 9th January, 1861 notes that he had disclosed his interest in the line, and also that the route for the line would have had the track passing through his back garden and within 35 ft of his house. He had had a word with the Engineer who had changed the route!

The same newspaper in its editorial for 23rd January complained of the secrecy surrounding the plans, and a letter, by "Civis", expressed doubts about the lack of public meetings and also over the route. He said that the Eastern route would give no real benefit to the town, however a route

Cap. cxx.
" The Bognor Railway Act, 1861."

Proposes the making of a Railway from the London, Brighton, and South Coast Railway, in the Parish of Eastergate in the County of Sussex, to the Town of Bognor in the Parish of Bersted otherwise South Bersted.

Incorporation of Acts, § 2.

Subscribers incorporated, with a Capital of 30,000*l.*, in Shares of 20*l.*, and with Power to borrow 10,000*l.*, §§ 3 to 7.

Power to enter into Traffic Arrangements with London and Brighton Railway Company, §§ 9 to 14.

Meetings : Directors, §§ 15 to 22.

Line of Railway, §§ 23, 24.

Two Years for Lands to be purchased by Compulsion, § 26.

Four Years for Completion of Railway, §§ 27, 28.

As to Communication with the London, Brighton, and South Coast Railway, §§ 32 to 36.

Power to the London, Brighton, and South Coast Railway Company to subscribe 5,000*l.*, § 37.

Land of the Proprietors of the Portsmouth and Arundel Navigation not to be taken without their Consent ; Easement provided, § 38.

Proprietors Rights and Privileges not to be prejudiced, § 39.

Mode of crossing the disused Portion of the Portsmouth and Arundel Navigation, § 40.

Tolls, §§ 41 to 50.

A summary of the main clauses of the Bognor Railway Act, 1861.

LONDON, BRIGHTON, AND SOUTH-COAST RAILWAY.

THE PUBLIC is respectfully informed that it is intended to OPEN THE NEW BOGNOR BRANCH LINE On the 1st of JUNE, 1864.

ON AND FROM THAT DATE THE PRESENT STATIONS at YAPTON AND WOODGATE WILL BE CLOSED.

The Trains will no longer call at either of them, and the business heretofore done there will be transferred to the New Stations at BARNHAM JUNCTION and at BOGNOR.

GEORGE HAWKINS,
Traffic Manager.

Brighton Terminus.
May 11th, 1864.

An advertisement in the *West Sussex Gazette* giving notice of the opening of the new branch.

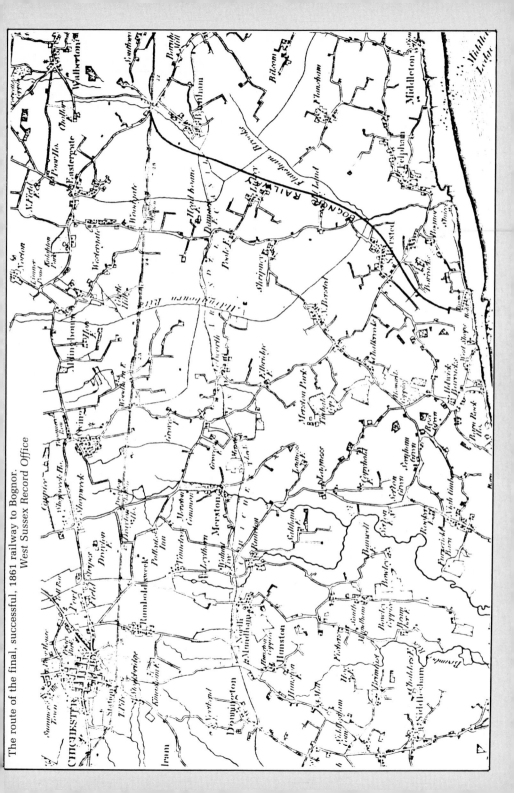

The route of the final, successful, 1861 railway to Bognor.
West Sussex Record Office

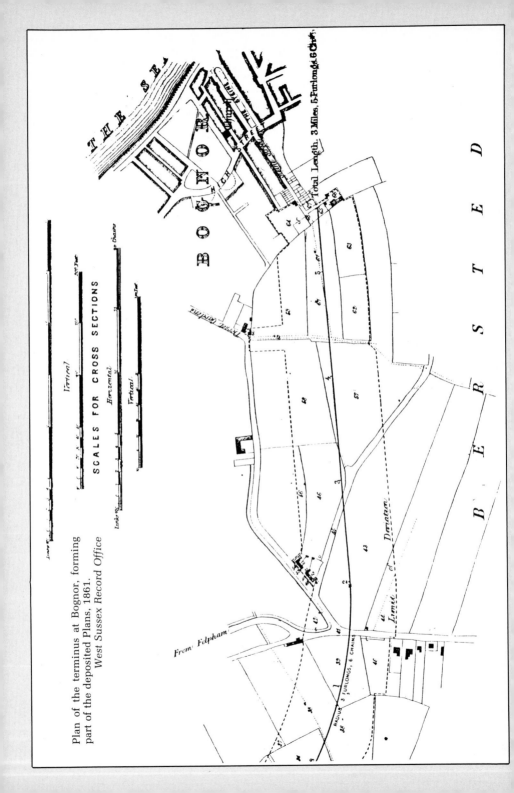

Plan of the terminus at Bognor, forming
part of the deposited Plans, 1861.
West Sussex Record Office

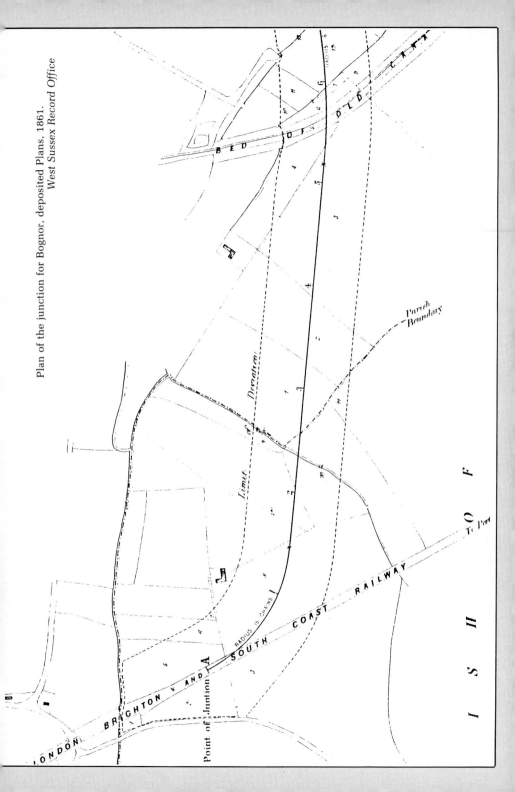

Plan of the junction for Bognor, deposited Plans, 1861.
West Sussex Record Office

A decorated farm wagon leads the Bognor Rifle Corps past The Sussex Hotel in a procession to celebrate the opening of the Branch Line, 1st June, 1864. This was drawn from life by a local art teacher, Brian Lomax.   *Gerard Young Collection*

Driver William King poses proudly on the footplate of No. 29 on the opening day at Barnham Junction, 1st June, 1864.   *R.W. Kidner Collection*

passing to the west of the station and going through the town would improve trade.

The *Journal* for 20th February contained a long article bemoaning the secrecy concerning the line ending with a claim that there was some form of collusion between the shareholders and the council, a brilliant deduction especially after the declared interest of the Mayor the previous month. The next week's paper included an article under the title of "A bold venture":

> The promoters of the Chichester, Midhurst and Bognor Railway have at last had a public meeting – not a hole in the corner affair, not a smug confab, but a real, honest, unmistakeable public meeting at – MIDHURST. No wonder the spire fell [a reference to the collapse of the Chichester Cathedral spire]. It was enough to bring down half the spires in Europe; it was so manly, so noble and English, so much in the style of, "who's afraid? here goes for a public meeting at – MIDHURST." And there is to be another one soon; may we all be there to see. But really now, to be more in earnest, is it not more hazardous to do these things more publicly. It is unquestionably dangerous at Chichester, and it may be so at Midhurst.

Not surprisingly with such fierce local opposition the attempt failed. It was not the last that Bognor folk heard from the indomitable Mr Bird for in 1863 he laid a further plan before Parliament. This was almost identical to the previous one except for the manner of crossing the main line at Chichester. This time it was to cross at right angles, with branch lines either side entering into Chichester station, thus enabling either a straight run from Bognor to Midhurst or to Chichester and vice versa. Again heavy opposition killed the idea.

Meanwhile in Bognor the years 1862 and 1863 had passed with no sign of the railway company doing any work on the line and hopes were fading. However on Saturday 18th April, 1863 a ceremony occurred which did something to buoy up the sinking spirits of the town. The *West Sussex Gazette* stated:

> A gay procession was formed by the Norfolk Hotel. The Rifle Corps, under Ensign Lomax, with the Worthing and Chichester bands played merrily.
> The procession, lead by Bognor fishermen, passed through the town and out to a field in Upper Bognor where was waiting a young lady, Miss Arnold of Romsey, who was to perform the ceremony of turning the first sod.

The article further noted that:

> A very nice barrow, made of mahogany, and a spade to match, had been prepared for the occasion. Miss Arnold raised a square of turf, and placed it in the barrow, which she wheeled along a plank, amid the deafening cheers of the onlookers.

The bands played "God Save The Queen", the Rev. E. Eedle, Vicar of South Bersted, said a few choice words and a prayer was offered up by the Rev. Edward Miller, Vicar of Bognor. The crowd then retired to the Assembly Rooms where a cold collation was laid out and champagne flowed freely. In the evening a Ball took place to celebrate the occasion, the outside of the Assembly Rooms was "brilliantly illuminated by Mr Wonham's device of the Star and Prince's Feathers, which had a very pretty effect". The massed bands played so loudly that they had to be removed to the other side of the

OPENING OF THE NEW RAILWAY FROM BARNHAM TO BOGNOR.—The long-talked-of railway from Barnham to Bognor was opened yesterday. On Saturday last Col. Yolland, the government inspector, passed over the line for the purpose of giving a certificate of its completeness. With the exception of one or two minor matters, the line was pronounced in an efficient state for working, and the trains commenced running for the conveyance of passengers and goods yesterday. The station accommodation, however, is as yet but very incomplete. The Bognor Terminus is situated near to the County Police Station, at the end of Dorset Gardens, and the shed adjoining is scarcely roofed in. This, however, will be all done in good time, and then Bognor will enjoy the full advantages to be derived from railway accommodation. The time table for this month will be seen advertised in our columns to day; and by it we learn that the distance from the Barnham Junction is completed in ten minutes, and a journey to the metropolis occupies but little over two hours. That there will be a great advantage to the place from this easy access one cannot doubt. The omnibus journey from Woodgate was a great drawback, and to accomplish this was more painful than the entire journey from London to Woodgate. Some little inconvenience will be felt by the closing of the Yapton and Woodgate Stations by those who live in the adjoining villages; but the great advantage given to Bognor by the opening of the new line cannot be too highly considered.

A report in the *West Sussex Gazette* describing the recent Board of Trade inspection of the branch, and the first timetable (*below*) from the same paper.

LONDON, BRIGHTON, AND SOUTH COAST RAILWAY.

OPENING OF THE BOGNOR BRANCH.

LOCAL TIME TABLE for JUNE, 1864, showing the Communications between Bognor and Portsmouth, Brighton and London.

DOWN. — Week Days.											
			1 2 3	1&2	1&2	1&2	Ex 1&2		1 2 3		
	a.m	a.m	a.m	a.m	a.m	p.m	p.m	p.m	p.m		
Kensington .... dep	..	..	..	9 32	1137	1 35	3 35	..	6 30	..	..
Victoria .... „	..	..	5 55	9 35	12 5	2 5	3 55	..	6 55	..	..
London Bridge ...... „	..	..	6 0	10 0	1210	2 10	4 5	..	7 0	..	..
			1 2 3	1&2	1&2	1&2	1&2		1 2 3		
Brighton .... dep.	..	..	8.25	1120	1 45	3 35	5 20	..	8 50	..	..
	1 2 3	1&2	1&2	1&2	1&2	1 2 3		1&2			
Portsmouth .... dep	5 40	8 5	8 40	1130	1 30	3 25	..	6 10	..	..	..
Barnham Junction.... dep.	6 40	8 55	9 35	1220	2 40	4 40	5 5	7 5	9 55	..	..
Bognor .... arr	6 50	9 5	9 45	1230	2 50	4 50	5 15	7 15	10 5	..	..

DOWN. — Sundays.									
		1 2 3	Exc 1 2 3	1&2				1 2 3	
	a.m	a.m	a.m	p.m	p.m	p.m	p.m	p.m	
Kensington .... dep	..	6 35	..	1255	..	..	..	5 35	..
Victoria .... „	..	6 55	8 0	1 15	..	..	..	5 30	..
London Bridge ...... „	..	7 0	8 0	1 20	..	..	..	6 35	..
		Exc 1 2 3	1 2 3	1 2 3				1 2 3	
Brighton .... dep.	..	8 55	9 25	3 10	..	..	..	8 25	..
	1 2 3			1 2 3	1 2 3	1 2 3	1 2 3		
Portsmouth .... dep	7 0	..	..	3 35	4 35	6 30	7 15	..	..
Barnham Junction.... dep.	7 55	9 55	1040	4 35	5 35	7 20	8 15	9 40	..
Bognor .... arr	8 5	10 5	1050	4 45	5 45	7 30	8 25	9 50	..

UP. — Week Days.											
	a.m	a.m	a.m	a.m	p.m	p.m	p.m	p.m	p.m		
Bognor .... dep	6 20	8 35	9 8	1148	2 0	4 5	5 35	6 45	9 35	..	..
Barnham Junction .... arr.	6 30	8 45	9 18	1155	2 10	4 15	5 45	6 55	9 45	..	..
			1 2 3	1&2	1&2	1&2	1&2		1 2 3		
Portsmouth .... arr.	..	..	1030	1245	3 23	5 20	6 25	..	1045	..	..
	1 2 3	1&2	1&2	1&2	1&2	1 2 3		1&2			
Brighton .... arr.	7 45	9 40	1035	1 20	3 20	5 40	..	7 50	..	..	..
	1 2 3	Ex 1&2	Ex 1&2	1&2	1&2	1 2 3		1&2			
London Bridge........ arr	9 25	11 0	1115	3 40	5 20	6 40	..	9 30	..	..	..
Victoria .... „	9 30	11 5	1120	3 45	5 25	6 50	..	9 55	..	..	..
Kensington .... „	1016	1137	1137	3 40	5 34	7 10	..	..	..	..	..

UP. — Sundays.									
	a.m	a.m	a.m	p.m	p.m	p.m	p.m	p.m	
Bognor .... dep	6 55	9 25	1015	3 45	5 15	6 55	7 50	8 50	..
Barnham Junction .... arr.	7 5	9 35	1025	3 55	5 25	7 5	8 0	9 0	..
		1 2 3	1 2 3	1 2 3				1 2 3	
Portsmouth .... arr.	..	1033	1136	4 50	..	..	..	10 0	..
	1 2 3			1 2 3		Exc 1 2 3	1 2 3		
Brighton .... arr.	8 15	..	..	5 45	..	8 5	9 20	..	..
	1 2 3				1 2 3	Exc 1 2 3	1&2		
London Bridge........ arr	1025	..	..	..	8 15	9 50	1110	..	..
Victoria .... „	1030	..	..	..	8 20	10 5	1115	..	..
Kensington .... „	11 4	..	..	..	8 40	..	..	..	..

All Trains 1st, 2nd, and 3rd Class, between Bognor and Barnham Junction.

GEO. HAWKINS,
Traffic Manager.

Terminus, Brighton,
27th May, 1864.

William Collins (a local youth) who spent 1st June, 1864 travelling between Barnham Junction and Bognor on the first, free, day of the Branch Line.   *B. Watson*

Another view of the opening day at Barnham Junction, William Collins is the boy third from the left, front row.   *Gerard Young Collection*

street! The entry in the company's minute book recorded that: "The proceedings gave universal satisfaction".

There were, however, still some doubts among the locals that this scheme should proceed further than any of the others put forward over the last 40 years. The local reporter for the *West Sussex Gazette* wrote only six days after the cutting the first sod ceremony that: "Some large holes were dug on the line to ascertain the quality of the soil which will have to be removed. This certainly strengthens the idea that ere long a reality may appear where a mere shadow has so long existed". And again on 5th May he says: "Some few hands are in active operation of the railway. We are told that about 200 will be employed next week, which may or may not come to pass exactly". Obviously the men were employed, and work did continue because his tone becomes softer and his writing shows a growing belief that here at last is a dream which will become a reality, and for the first time, in June 1863, he refers to it as "our railway". In July a glowing report appears in his paper:

> Our railway operations proceed with vigour, the same kind of labour as was imposed on the ancient Israelites by their tyranical masters, the Egyptians, is at present being carried on with active energy at this end of the line, to supply materials for the erection of the various required buildings.

The land over which the line was to pass was relatively flat, and there being few natural obstructions, work on the track laying and station building appeared to be quickly reaching a conclusion, so much so that in August 1863 the local reporter wrote "this branch is expected to be opened on the 30th of September". This was somewhat premature, however, as the trackwork was not completed until May 1864. Fourteen months after construction work had begun Colonel Yolland, the Board of Trade Inspector, passed over the line to check its completeness, and apart from a few minor details saw no reason why it should not open on the advertised date, 1st June, 1864.

Barnham Junction station, although only half a mile from the village of that name, was in fact in the Parish of Eastergate. It was one mile thirty chains west of Yapton station and one mile twenty chains east of Woodgate. The brick station house, built by Jabez Reynolds at a cost of £899, was on the up side of the "West Coast Line". A spur off the up line led to a wooden goods shed, taken from the now closed Yapton station and rebuilt behind the up platform, to the west of the station building. A smaller spur to the east led to the cattle dock. The down platform was extra wide as the south face of it served the Bognor branch line. A large canopy covered not only the down main and the branch line, but also the track of the branch. The track layout was such that it precluded direct running on to the Bognor line except from the direction of Chichester – and then only by shunting, and so passengers for further afield had to detrain for connections to London, Brighton or Portsmouth. Turntable facilities for the branch line locomotives were provided on a track to the west of the down platform and between the main and branch lines.

The line, surveyed by Fuller and Company of Chichester and engineered by Robert Jacomb Hood, left the branch platform on a left hand curve at a radius of 15 chains for one and a half furlongs, the line then straightened out for half a mile followed by another left hand curve of 6 furlongs radius for half a mile. A very short straight was followed by a right hand curve of 30 chains length at 80 chains radius. A length of straight, or very slight right hand curve, took the line almost to the terminus where two left hand curves of 25 and 40 chains radius respectively took it in to the Bognor station.

The station was situated to the east of the County Police station, and west of Circus Road (now Ockley Road) on the northern edge of Dorset Gardens. The line was 3 miles and 46 chains long and had 10 under-bridges for the many streams and ditches it had to cross, the largest of which were the moribund Portsmouth and Arundel canal, by this time a dried up gash across the countryside, and the Aldingbourne Rife. Clauses 38 and 40 of the Bognor Railway Act were inserted to protect the interests of the canal company. Clause 38 states:

> The (Bognor Railway) Company shall, in the event of the said Navigation being required for use by Water Traffic, or if the same shall be converted into a Road or Railway, raise the level of the Railway 5 feet above the levels shown on the deposited section, and shall carry the same by a swing bridge across the said Navigation, Road or Railway and further shall open the said Swing Bridge at all times for the passage of traffic lawfully conveyed on such Navigation, Road or Railway.

Clause 40 goes on to say that there would be a £10 fine on every occasion that the swing bridge impedes canal traffic, but as there was no water there could not logically be any canal traffic so the Bognor Company wisely saved its money and built a straightforward steel girder bridge.

Gradients on the flat coastal plain were slight, the steepest being only 1 in 230 and 1 in 550. Only one level crossing was needed, this being at the northern extremity of the Bognor station yard where the line crossed the Bersted Road (now Chichester Road) next to the Richmond Arms public house. Two footbridges spanned the line, one at the aforementioned level crossing and the other a couple of hundred yards further on to allow the footpath from South Bersted to Felpham to cross the line. One road bridge was erected a few years after the line was opened to carry the newly extended Highfield Road over the track. The contractors, Jackson & Bissett were paid £22,500 for laying the line.

Bognor station was provided with a single platform 550 ft long, and canopied for 190 ft of its length. Four sidings lay in a direct line westwards from the platform and goods facilities were provided by a large brick goods shed. A spur line off the main line gave access to the cattle and carriage docks to the north of the platform, and the same line also led to a 45 ft turntable and a two-road clap board-built engine shed.

The station building was of simple clap board construction with brick ends. It had a lavatory and a small lamp room on the western side, separate ladies, 1st class and general waiting rooms in the centre and booking office, porters' room and boiler room to the east.

A small station signal box to the rear of the platform controlled the running lines and goods yard and a further signal box was positioned to the north of the Bersted Road level crossing to control the gates and the single line track.

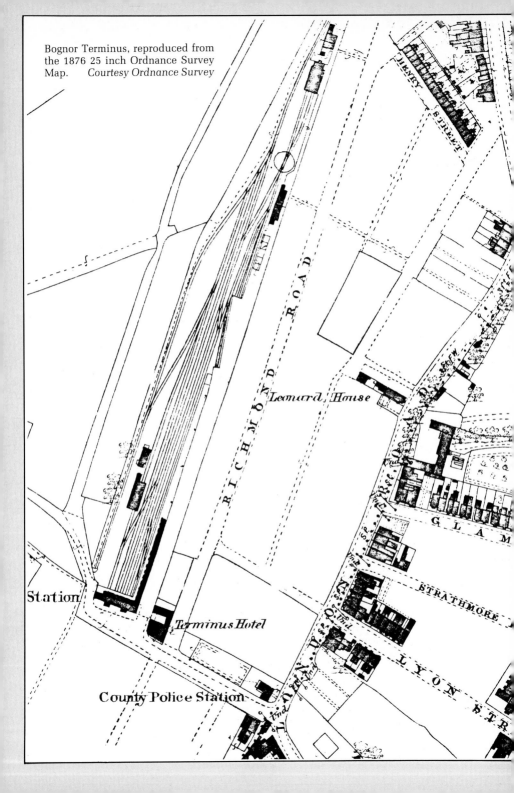

Bognor Terminus, reproduced from
the 1876 25 inch Ordnance Survey
Map.   *Courtesy Ordnance Survey*

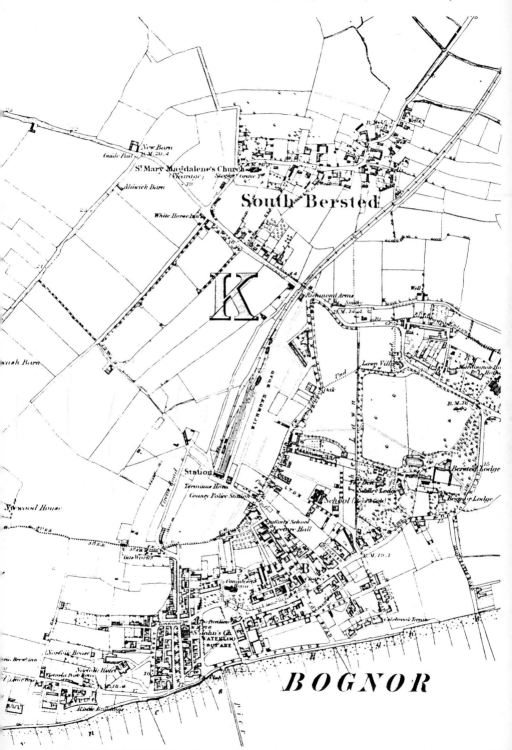

Part of the 6″, 1880 Ordnance Survey Map of Bognor Regis. *Courtesy Ordnance Survey*

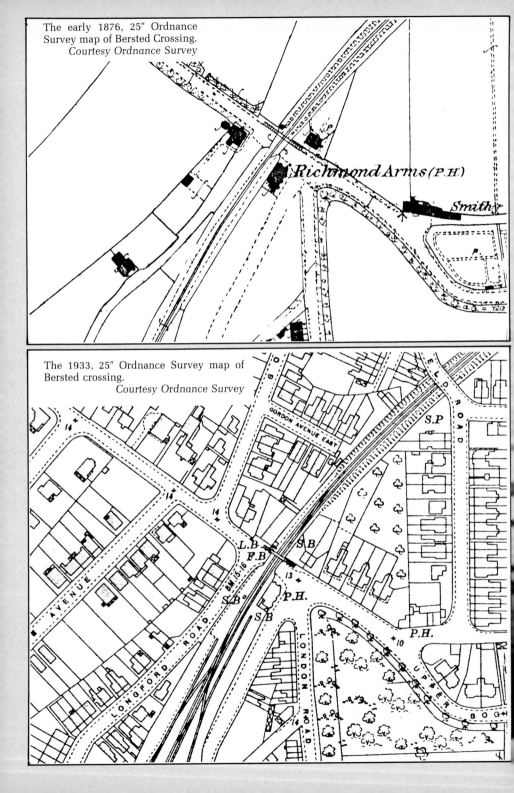

The early 1876, 25″ Ordnance Survey map of Bersted Crossing.
Courtesy Ordnance Survey

Richmond Arms (P.H.)

Smithy

The 1933, 25″ Ordnance Survey map of Bersted crossing.
Courtesy Ordnance Survey

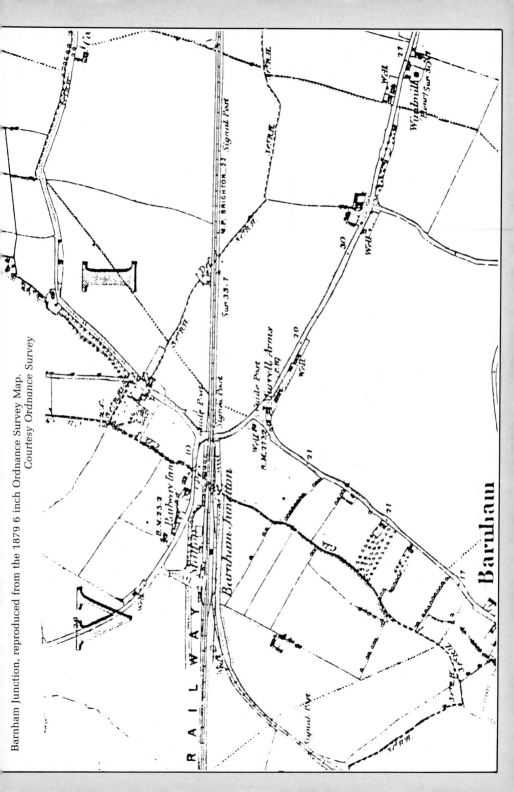

Barnham Junction, reproduced from the 1879 6 inch Ordnance Survey Map.
Courtesy Ordnance Survey

Wednesday 1st June dawned clear and bright, and the new stations of Barnham Junction and Bognor opened and the now redundant Woodgate closed. Flags flew from windows of shops and houses in the town and a procession, led by a gaily decorated farm waggon filled with townspeople, passed through the streets.

The first train left Bognor on its ten minute journey to Barnham, hauled by an old Sharp-Roberts 2–2–2, No. 29, built in 1845. In Bognor the shops had closed and a public holiday was declared. The report in the *West Sussex Gazette* states: "Bognor will enjoy the full advantage to be derived from railway accomodation . . . that there will be a great advantage to this place from the easy access one cannot doubt", and continues, "The Omnibus journey from Woodgate was a great drawback, and to accomplish this was more painful than the entire journey from London to Woodgate".

Shortly after 3 pm the train left Barnham Junction, the Bognor Rifle Corps, having led the parade in Bognor, and then marched to Barnham, played the train out. On returning to the Bognor terminus the Directors and their guests left the station for a luncheon at the Assembly Rooms, and the inhabitants of the two towns enjoyed free rides for the rest of the afternoon.

The first timetable shows us that there were nine return trains on a weekday and eight on Sundays. All three classes of accommodation, 1st, 2nd and 3rd, were available on all but a few of the journeys.

For the first two months of its life the Bognor Railway ran its own affairs, then on 29th July, 1864 the LB & SCR took over the running of the line. It did not however cease to be a privately owned line until 11th January, 1871 when the Brighton company paid the final instalment of the purchase price and the Bognor Railway Company was dissolved.

In 1874, after many complaints about the simple wooden terminus, the company added a front porch under which passengers could shelter whilst waiting for an omnibus or a cab.

July 1874 also saw the first through train running between Victoria and Bognor, although some shunting was required at Barnham. The train left Victoria at 12.35 pm, reaching Bognor at 2.50. The return left Bognor at 3.15 pm arriving Victoria at 5.30. From 1877 a Sunday train was put on leaving Victoria at 7.05 am and, after joining a London Bridge portion at East Croydon, it ran through to Bognor via Crawley calling at most stations on the way. After remaining at Bognor all day the train left for Victoria at 6 pm.

Barnham Junction had its first signal box from 1876, a 42 lever box situated to the west of the station next to the up main line.

1878 saw the laying of a new siding in the Bognor yard, to the north of the goods shed. A further siding was added in 1885. As a result of the popularity of the seaside town the railway company laid on Saturday excursion trains from 1887.

Also in 1887 a new line was laid at Ford Junction which allowed direct running from Littlehampton to Brighton or Arundel without having to reverse at Ford as was previously the case. And so in later years, as will be described, direct running was possible from Bognor on to the main line, thus allowing trains to run a coastal service from Bognor to Brighton via Littlehampton.

Chapter Four
Wind and Fire

Bognor, being a seaside resort which made its living mostly from holiday makers in the summer season, depended on the railways as the only mass transportation system at this time. So when changes were made in the timetable for the benefit of the town they were eagerly reported in the local paper. The *Bognor Observer* for Wednesday 1st June, 1892 has one such report under the heading of "Railway Facilities":

> Among the alterations in the local railway time-table for June is the re-introduction of the London and Portsmouth cheap trains on Saturday and Tuesday, one of which leaving Victoria at 1 pm, calls at Barnham Junction for Bognor which is reached at 2.58, the journey being thus effected in less than two hours. This train, especially on Saturday, will no doubt be appreciated during the season by city gentlemen who come down for the Sunday by the sea-side.

1892 saw the beginning of seven years bad luck for Bognor station, as during the winter of that year the first of its misfortunes occurred. During a fierce gale, part of the "wooden shack" that was the station, collapsed. The building was not demolished as was the wish of the townsfolk however, and the old building was simply re-erected as before.

This was not to be the last time that the elements were to have a disastrous effect on the old wooden station, because on the night of Tuesday 2nd March, 1897 gale force winds were again blowing the length and breadth of the south coast. The strongest recorded winds for 50 years struck Bognor overnight. All night the wind howled round the town, fences blew over, chimney stacks fell crashing to the streets below and sheds and lean-to's fell in heaps on the ground. At 10.30 on the morning of Wednesday the 3rd, (with a loud crash) when the winds were at their severest, the canopy over Bognor's only platform collapsed. The thick wooden supports holding up the canopy had snapped like matchsticks, with the majority of the debris falling on the track alongside the platform, effectively closing the station to passenger traffic.

None of the other station buildings suffered any damage. However, at Barnham station a portion of the canopy overhanging the Bognor platform was blown off. The damage was not as severe as that at Bognor and there was no disruption to the trains using the main line.

That some good might come from the destruction of the canopy at Bognor station was the fervent hope of the local reporter for the *Bognor Observer*, who wrote: "The only solace to Bognor residents from the devastation is the damage to the railway station, which we hope will now be made of a character befitting a seaside town". This was wishful thinking however as the debris was soon cleared up and the canopy rebuilt as before.

Photographs of the damage were taken by Mr F. Reynolds and were used by the national newspapers; copies of the pictures were put on sale locally and were quickly sold out.

The desire for a larger, more imposing terminus did not have to wait too long for fulfilment. The LB&SCR had a large number of new plans in hand and in 1899 under the heading of the LB&SCR, (*Various Powers*) Act the

Local children pose amongst the wreckage of the station canopy destroyed in the gale of 3rd May, 1897. The much maligned 'wooden shack' is exposed in all its glory.
Gerard Young Collection

Inquisitive locals have an unusual view of the platform following the March gale of 1897. On the left hand side is the imposing goods shed and the Station signal box can be seen at the end of the platform. Above the goods wagons can be seen a row of bathing machines stored for the winter. *Gerard Young Collection*

company had included two plans of local interest. The first of the plans showed the enlargement of Barnham Junction to include for the first time direct running from the main line onto the Bognor branch. The second was more important to prestige-hungry Bognor: it showed that the area of the terminus was to be almost doubled, two more platforms would be added and a large goods yard was to be built to the south of the passenger area. The most important item however was the replacement of the old wooden station building by a large, imposing, brick-built station house.

As the reporter for the *Bognor Observer* put it: "The plan of the LB & SCR company for their new station at Bognor, as will be seen by reference to the plan, shows in a very satisfactory manner the opinion of the company as to the future of the town". He continues, "The yard provides accomodation for 234 waggons which will give an indication of the intended area". However, he goes on to say, "we trust that when Bognor station is completed the company will turn their attention to Barnham Junction. At present there is not a square foot of the roof which does not leak in wet weather, whilst the wretched waiting room accomodation is about as cold and dreary as can be imagined".

The Bill went before the Parliamentary committee on Friday 30th June and was unopposed due to a deal between the Brighton company and the Grosvenor Hotel, by which the company purchased the lease from the Hotel; they already owned the land. It was fortunate that such plans were in hand to replace the old station as in the early hours of the morning of Saturday 29th October, 1899 the entire building was burnt to the ground.

At 1.25 am P.C.'s Welch and Ireland in company with a Coastguard were patrolling along the sea front when they noticed a glow in the centre of the town. Quickly realising that there was a fire at the railway station the two P.C.'s split up and raced off to raise the alarm. P.C. Ireland ran to the fire station to ring the fire alarm and P.C. Welch made haste to rouse the station master, Mr Gillham. On his way he passed the station and saw flames bursting through the roof over the porters' room. Having roused Mr Gillham, P.C. Welch then ran back to the station which he had left only moments before; however on his return he saw the flames had taken a good hold of the wooden building and were now attacking the ticket office. He then ran and woke the booking clerk who quickly raced to the scene and burst open the door to the ticket office intent on saving what he could. The room was full of smoke and so he was unable to get in and all was lost in the ensuing conflagration.

Meanwhile P.C. Ireland had woken Lt Stuart, the fire chief, who sent round messengers to rouse the other firemen. Lt Stuart took only eight minutes from the time the bell first rang to reach the Fire Station and start moving the truck with the hose reels on it to the railway station.

Mr Naldret, a Station Road shopkeeper, had roused the station porter, Mr Ethridge and he and his sons hurried to the now blazing station to see what could be done. He and the firemen arrived at about the same time and he had the firemen play their hoses on the waiting room while he entered the burning building, managing to recover some commercial baggage. Know-

Bognor station staff glumly inspect the remains of the platform canopy following one of the worst winter storms the town had ever seen. *Gerard Young Collection*

Members of the Bognor volunteer fire brigade begin the clear-up after unsuccessfully fighting the fire at Bognor station in the early hours of the morning of 29th October, 1899. *Gerard Young Collection*

ing also where the cast-iron safe was located, he had the firemen keep the area wet and later, when the fire had subsided a little, he and another porter, Mr King, managed to pull it free from the flames by means of ropes with hooks on the ends.

By this time the building was on fire from end to end, a lead gas pipe had melted and the gas ignited, flaring for upwards of 20 minutes before the main was located and the gas supply turned off. Fifteen or twenty feet of the new platform canopy was destroyed as were the advertising boards under them. The bookstall of W.H. Smith and Sons was also destroyed but the manager, Mr Mitchel, managed to save his account books. The station master and a gang of men pushed away some carriages and goods trucks which were standing at the buffers and in imminent danger of being consumed by the fire.

By 4 am the fire was almost out, but not before the station building had been totally gutted. The only things left standing were the brick chimneys and a small portion of the lamp room. All the station account books, tickets, and parcels in the booking office were destroyed, as were four bicycles, the remains of which were found in the ashes at daybreak.

Dawn brought with it a dismal scene of destruction, the crowd gathered at the site had a clear view from the station approach road right through to the track beyond. A gang of men under the supervision of inspector Morris, from Havant, first put up a hoarding blocking off the view and then set to work building a temporary station master's office under what was left of the platform canopy. By Monday morning the work was completed, a goods van having been converted into a makeshift booking office. The unfortunate Mr Mitchel however had to conduct the business of W.H. Smith from one of the station benches. No firm cause for the conflagration was found but one theory was that coats left to dry over a stove in the porters' room had ignited and set fire to the rest of the room. This view is supported by the fact that when P.C. Welch first reached the scene, it was from the porters' room that the first flames were seen.

"The End" for the wooden station building at Bognor following the disastrous fire of Saturday 29th October, 1899. *Gerard Young Collection*

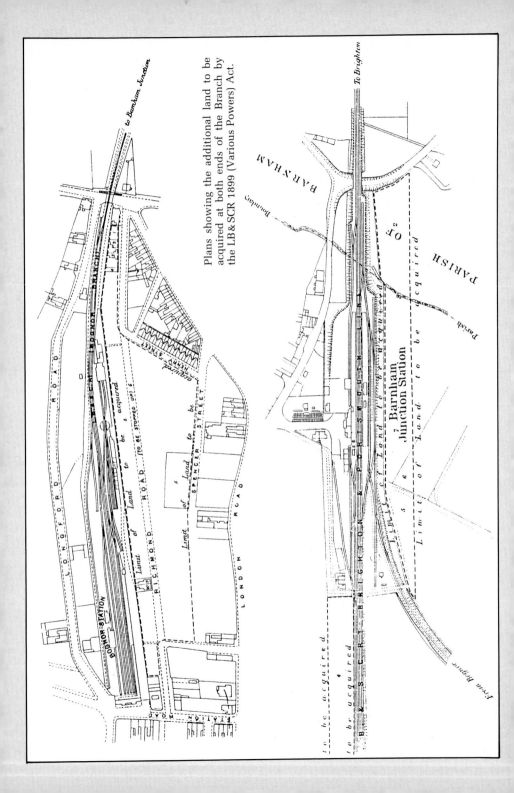

Plans showing the additional land to be acquired at both ends of the Branch by the LB&SCR 1899 (Various Powers) Act.

Chapter Five
Reconstruction

The years 1899 to 1902 saw much activity in the Bognor Terminus as the old station was swept away. The remains of the station building were demolished and work started on the new construction, track work was lifted and the new plans realised. This new track layout was similar in shape to the bottom half of an hour glass; the western half held the passenger accommodation with three platforms. Between the tracks for platforms two and three there was a third line which enabled the engine to run-round its train, the points being controlled by a Saxby & Farmer ground frame behind the buffers. The eastern half of the station was devoted solely to goods and coal sidings.

Richmond Road had been stopped up and on the site of the old road were now two sidings, adjacent to which were a further two sidings and a new cattle dock. A double track led off from the top end of these sidings to the goods shed which stood beside Spencer Street. In the angle formed by Henry and Spencer Streets were a further three sidings with coal staithes for the use of the Bognor Coal and Transport Company Ltd, now part of Corrals.

During the rebuilding old covered goods wagons were utilized as temporary offices and passengers encountered some discomfort and inconvenience, but all this was accepted with good humour. The plans for the new station received almost universal approval, the only setback being when the refreshment room had its license turned down. Work on the new station accommodation had just started in October 1900 and a drinks license was applied for "at a house and premises proposed to be erected by the LB & SCR on a piece of land abutting the western boundary of the existing Bognor station goods yard, and about 50 ft south of the southern most end of the goods shed". The application was heard in the Magistrates Court in September and was opposed by the licensee of the Railway Hotel. The court found in favour of the objectors and the license was withheld.

By 1902 the new station building was complete. Built of brick at a cost of £37,000 it contained a large booking hall, parcels office, ladies waiting room, refreshment rooms and a first floor residence for the station master, all topped off with a large clock tower. A large covered concourse, with a hard wearing floor of Stuarts Granolithic, held a book stall and a fruit kiosk as well as a small cabin for the use of the cab drivers whilst waiting for a fare.

The new brick engine shed, however, was not completed until 1903 and was built on the site of the old wooden structure with a new goods shed, also of brick, being built on the eastern side of the newly acquired land and completed in the previous year (1902).

The station signal box was closed and a new 80 lever box was opened adjacent to the engine shed; the Bersted Crossing signal box was retained with a re-locked frame. As well as all this the line was doubled from the terminus to the Bersted Crossing to facilitate shunting within the complex. The work was carried out by W. Johnson and Company of Wandsworth, total cost of the re-build being £68,000.

Meanwhile at Barnham Junction land was purchased to build more sidings; the first was to the west of the station on the up side and the second was to the south of the Bognor branch line. At the same time replacement of the old slotted post signals was begun, the work being completed in December 1904 at a reported cost of £15,000. In 1905 a new 55 ft turntable was installed in front of the engine shed at Bognor to help with the increasing traffic loads and larger locomotives.

The Bank Holiday Act of 1871 provided the railways with a ready supply of day trippers to bolster the normal annual traffic, and cheap tickets meant that trains to the coast were packed. By the early 1900s day trips had caught on to such an extent that complete Sunday Schols or factories packed up and moved *en masse* to the sea side for a day out.

Bognor had its fair share of these trippers, so many in fact that in 1907 Bognor town council considered petitioning the railway company to stop the excursions for the month of August. The *Bognor Observer* for Wednesday 17th July carried a report of the town council meeting at which it had been said that the excursionists were ruining the town for those who came to the coast for longer holidays with their families. Furthermore, hawkers from London were coming in with the day trippers and selling their wares on the platform before the visitors had chance to look round the town and make their purchases from the *bona fide* local tradesmen. The resolution was put to the vote, and on the Chairman's casting vote, it was lost.

A look at the LB&SCR Special Traffic Notice for week ending 22nd June, 1907 shows just how many party visitors there were:

16th June   National Sunday League, 800
17th June   Thomas Cook and Sons, 500
18th June   St George's and Christ Church Sunday Schools, 700
              All Saints' Sunday School, 600
              Trinity Sunday School, 175
19th June   Wallington Sunday School, 650
              St Peter's Presbyterian Sunday School, 900
              Miss Hemming's Party, 120
20th June   Miss Watney's Party, 350
              Emmanuel Church Sunday School, 400
              Restalls Excursion, 800
              Miss Nicholson's Party, 30

This made a total of 5935 day trippers, a number which does not include those travelling by scheduled trains.

Over the next few years it became apparent that with the large volume of traffic at Bognor, the ludicrous situation of a large terminus at the end of a single line with no direct access to the main line could not continue. So in January 1911 work began to double the track between Bersted Crossing and Barnham Junction, not without some bad feeling between the work force and management. As the reporter for the *Chichester Observer* put it,

A mild form of strike took place among the Navvies engaged in doubling the branch line between Barnham Junction and Bognor. Discontent has been manifest since operations commenced a week or two ago at the rate of pay, which is 4½d. per hour. Representations have been made for an increase, but nothing satisfactory resulted. The men came out for a demand of 5d. per hour. The engineer in charge was approached and by dint of persuasion he succeded in getting the men to

Bognor station staff pose for the camera shortly after the opening of the new station in 1902. The station master, George Gilham, is seated third from the left.

Gerard Young Collection

George Gilham sits with other members of his staff who were not available for the first photograph seen above. *Gerard Young Collection*

resume work until the arrival of the chief engineer from London. At the time of going to press we learn that the men are still working and that the chief engineer is not expected until evening.

An answer to the problem was obviously found as work continued without further trouble.

At Barnham the track layout was extensively remodelled and a double junction was incorporated on the western end of the station to allow direct running from the branch to the main line for the first time in 47 years. The 1876 signal box was closed and a new one built on the end of the island platform. Work was completed by 30th July, 1911.

As previously stated, changes in the junction layout at Ford in 1887 enabled direct running to and from Littlehampton by any one of three routes – Brighton, Arundel and Ford or vice versa. In 1911 when Bognor trains were able to do likewise on to the main line, a motor-train service was instituted. This service was run by specially adapted 'D1' class engines with a single carriage attached. The engine and carriage were linked by a pneumatic control system which enabled the driver to sit in a cab in the carriage and drive the train, whilst the fireman stayed on the footplate and fed and watered the engine in the usual way.

The motor-train service from Bognor was a local coastal service and the 1912 timetable showed 10 trains per day leaving for Littlehampton, calling at Barnham and Ford, with one of these carrying on from Littlehampton to Brighton; the service was 3rd class only.

The popularity of Bognor with day trippers continued and between 9th and 11th July, 1913, 7779 day tickets were sold by the railway company. At Easter 1918 trains were so full that some intending passengers were left on the platform at Victoria. Thomas Cook's reported that for two weeks in July there were 10,000 visitors and for the last week there were 35,000. It must be remembered that at this time the population of Bognor was only 8500.

Following World War I the class barriers began to fall and this was reflected by the railway companies. The early post-war timetables show the introduction of 3rd class Pullman cars on the Victoria–Bognor route. At first old American 1st class cars were used, but later former wartime ambulance trains from the GWR, L&YR and LNWR were converted for this purpose.

A motor-train propelled by class 'D1' No. 297 pulls into Bognor station in February 1927. The driver controlled the train from a cab in the front carriage whilst the fireman stayed on the footplate.   *R.M. Casserley*

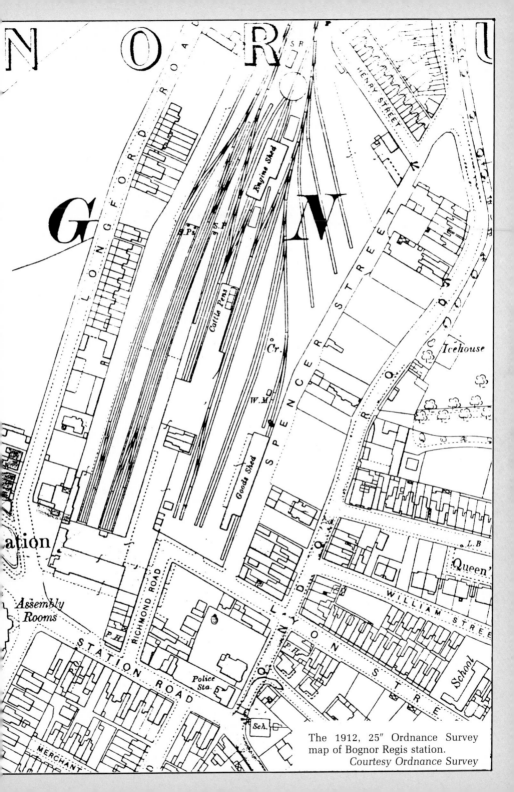

The 1912, 25″ Ordnance Survey map of Bognor Regis station.
Courtesy Ordnance Survey

Railway carriages finally make it on to the Brooklands! (the proposed terminus for the 1845 Bognor Branch Railway). These old Stroudley four-wheelers were turned into holiday homes in about 1910. *Author's Collection*

Station Road, Bognor in August 1925; the large crowds would indicate a train has just arrived at the station which lies behind the tall trees. *Author's Collection*

THE RAILWAY STATION · BOGNOR.

The elegant new station at Bognor with its imposing clock tower, c.1904. The fore-court was soon spoiled by a row of shops along the line of the brick wall.

Gerard Young Collection

UP.	From BOGNOR to LONDON—DAILY.																						SUNDAYS.	
BOGNOR ......(dep)	7 30 7 48	8 30	9 10 9 39	1025 1055	12 0 1 55 2 25	3 27	4 40 5 20	6 43 7 17 7 50	9 25 6 50 7 35 9 45 1015	......	6 30 6 38 8 0	9 0 9 45											
Bernham Jun (arr)	7 38 7 55		9 17 9 47	1033 11 3 12 8 2	3 2 40 8 36	4 48 5 27 6 50 7 25 7 58	9 33 6 58 7 43 0 53 1023	......	6 37 6 46 8 8	9 8 9 54													
Lonoon Bridge ,	1023 9 50 1038 1050	......	1235 1 45 3 15	......	4 33	...... 7 35	......	1014 1247	......	1027	......		8 50 9 32											
VICTORIA ... ,,	1080 1065	......	...... 1240 1 53 2 37	......	4 42	...... 7 38	......	10 7 1255	......	1032	......		8 44 9 42											
† not on Saturdays.																								

DOWN.	From LONDON to BOGNOR—DAILY.																		SUNDAYS.	
VICTORIA......	6 20	......	8 0 1137 1030	......	1 42	......	3 57	......	4 55	......	7 20	......	8 20 9 0	1 15	......	6 30		
Lonoon Bridge	6 35	......	8 0 1135 1025	......	1255 1 50	......	4 0 4 55 5 0	......	......	7 25	......	......	8 30 8 55	1 28	......	6 40		
Barnham Junc.	8 8 8 55 9 25	1042 1120	2 11 1247 2 43 2 58	3 48 4 22	4 55 5 59 6 81	6 57 7 32	8 10 9 42	16 / 8 3 10 2 1052	......	4 47 6 48 8 15	9 17 10 0							
BOGNOR	6 15 9 3	9 33	1050 1123	2 19 1255 2 50 3 5 3 51	4 30 5 3	6 7 6 38	7 4 7 40	8 18 9 50 1015 8 11	1019 11 0 1115	4 55 6 56 8 33	9 25 10 8									
* Via Brighton.	† not on Saturdays.																			

UP.	From BOGNOR to LITTLEHAMPTON and BRIGHTON.																SUNDAYS.	
BOGNOR.............(dep.)	7 30	......	8 30 9 39	1025 1055	12 0 1 55 2 25	......	4 5 5 20	......	6 43 7 17 7 50 9 25	......	6 50 7 35 9 45	......	4 15 8 0				
LITTL'HMPTO (arr.)	8 12	......	9 5 10 5	......	1125 1252	......	3 7	......	4 50 6 0	......	7 40 8 5 8 28 10 7	......	7 25 8 5 1030	......	5 13 8 54	
BRIGHTON ,,	8 36	......	9 49 1051 1153	......	1 30 8 16	......	......	5 80	......	8 13 8 50	......	1040'	9 15 ......11 3'	......	5 50 9 10	
Mondays only.																		

DOWN.	From BRIGHTON and LITTLEHAMPTON to BOGNOR.																SUNDAYS.	
BRIGHTON ......(dep.)	......	7 10	......	8 50	......	1015 1135 1 20	......	3 55	......	6 0 6 25 5 22	......	8 55	......	7 0 9 35 3 30	......	8 50	
LITTL'HAMPTON ,,	......	7 42	......	5 20 9 25	......	1050 1215 2 0	2 42	4 15 5 30	6 22 7 0 6 25	9 20	......	7 45 9 55 4 5	......	8 49 9 36		
BOGNOR ....(arr.)	......	8 15	......	9 4 10 3	......	1128 1255 2 50	3 5 5 36	7 7 27 40	.. ..9 50 10 15	......	......	8 11 11 0 4 55	......	9 25 10 8	
† not on Saturdays.																		

Timetable for 18th November, 1903.

'B4' class No. 53 stands gleaming in the morning sun outside Bognor locomotive shed, February 1927. *R.M. Casserley*

Woodgate station, opened in 1846 and closed in 1864. Seen here in December 1983, it has been little-changed by successive owners. *Author*

Woodgate crossing in 1910, the 1846 crossing keeper's cottage is still on the right. A steam roller pauses outside the Prince of Wales Inn, having just crossed the main Portsmouth to Brighton line.

B. Watson

Bersted crossing at the turn of the century, the crossing keeper poses in front of the typical LB&SCR straight bar gates. To the right can just be seen the 1864 signal box that was demolished in 1938.

Gerard Young Collection

Woodgate crossing in 1983, the crossing keeper's cottage has changed little in its 137 years of existence. The Brighton-type gates have been replaced by the southern railway style, themselves replaced in turn by lifting barrier type operated by remote control from Chichester. *Author's Collection*

Barnham Junction in 1878. No. 214, *Seaford*, runs-round its train in the Bognor bay. In the foreground can be seen the tracks which allowed trains to enter the branch from the main line. *Author's Collection*

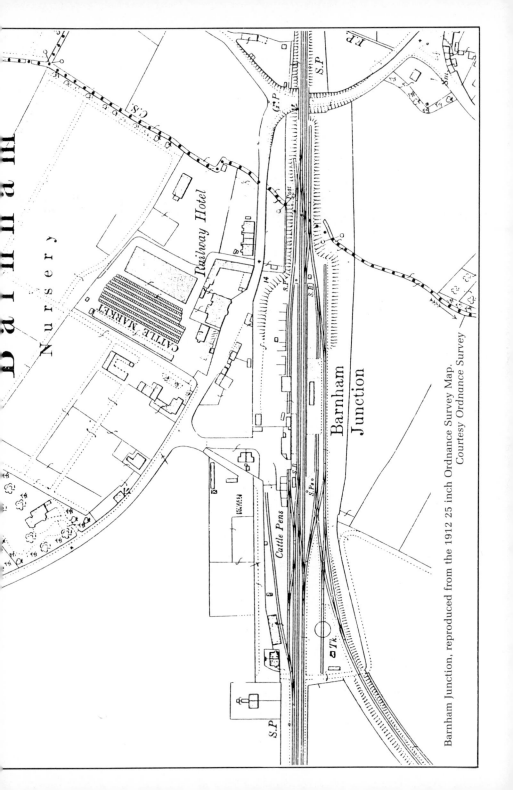

Barnham Junction, reproduced from the 1912 25 inch Ordnance Survey Map.
Courtesy Ordnance Survey

'B1' class No. 200, *Beresford*, stands at Barnham Junction with a Portsmouth-bound express, *c.*1890.   *Author's Collection*

Barnham Junction shortly after completion of the new island platform signal box in 1911. Note the LB&SCR ground signal in the foreground.   *Author's Collection*

"Gladstone" class No. 220, *Hampden*, with a Portsmouth express on the main line at Barnham Junction, while in the branch line bay an "A1" "Terrier" has just run-round its train. The "LV" (last vehicle) plate has yet to be transferred to the other end of the train; *c.*1904. *R.W. Kidner Collection*

Façade of the new Barnham station building; built in 1936 it is on a lower level to the platforms and is joined to them by a covered walkway and a subway to the island platform. Photographed in 1988, it can be seen that BR has allowed the building to become a little run-down. *Author*

Chapter Six
Grouping and Nationalisation

After almost five years of war the railways were in a sorry state. Repair work had been held over to the end of the war and by then the railway companies were short of men and most of all, money. Apart from Nationalisation the only solution the authorities could support was the wholesale amalgamation of the railway system into four "super companies". On 1st January, 1923 the LB&SCR, LSWR and SER were joined by government order into the Southern Railway, the ex-LB&SCR portion being known as the Central Division. Among the first changes was that the old LSWR route from Waterloo to Portsmouth was chosen as the main line and the rival LB&SCR Mid Sussex Line was used almost exclusively for Bognor expresses.

In 1928, Olby's (a well known local firm of builders merchants) took over a wharf at Bognor station. This consisted of a shed for storage of cement and the manufacture of breeze blocks, later the wharf was used to store timber. In 1939 the firm took over two railway cottages adjacent to the wharf for their expanding timber business.

King George the Fifth caught a chill in November 1928 which affected his right lung, and by December his condition was grave. Following an operation on 12th December the King showed signs of improvement. On 22nd January, 1929 an announcement from Buckingham Palace stated that, "the time is approaching when his Majesty's removal to sea air will be advantageous". Later on the same day a further announcement stated that the king would be recouperating at Craigwell House at Aldwick, a mile from Bognor. The King arrived at Bognor on Saturday 9th February having travelled down from London by ambulance. Special trains were laid on to carry royal visitors and government papers from Victoria to Bognor.

On 15th May the King, fully restored, left Bognor, again by motor ambulance. The Town Council applied to the King for the royal appendage "Regis" to the town's name; approval followed in June and so the town, and the railway station, became Bognor Regis.

As the old King lay dying in January 1936 his doctor told him not to worry as he would soon be in Bognor recovering; the King opened his eyes, looked at his doctor and said "Bu...r Bognor!" and promptly expired.

Although Bognor station was at its busiest in the summer months, it was by no means dead in the off-season. In 1931 the day started with the 5.18 am to Chichester, and 32 more trains came and went before the arrival of the last train at 11.10 pm. Of these 34 trains, 17 were local connecting to Brighton or Portsmouth; 4 of these made connections with an advertised service from Ashford (Kent) to Portsmouth, which was not a through train but a series of well-timed connections. The rest comprised 5 trains or connections from Horsham only, 3 from London Bridge via Horsham and 1 via Crawley; 5 from Victoria via Horsham and 1 via Crawley; 1 from Victoria via Hove and 1 from London Bridge via Brighton. Only one train contained Pullman cars, the 5.22 pm arrival from Victoria, part of which went on from Barnham to Chichester. The Pullmans spent the night at Bognor. This was the weekday service; on Saturdays there were some useful trains in the afternoon from

Bognor Regis station yard as seen from the Bersted Crossing footbridge. In this 1967 view the complete layout can be seen with the coal and goods sidings off to the left, the four platforms in the centre and the carriage sidings to the right. *Mowat Collection*

The signal box at the entrance to Bognor Regis station yard. Built in 1938 this 66 lever box replaced both the Station and Crossing boxes. Constructed in the then popular 'Odeon' style it is in stark contrast with the traditional design of the Barnham signal box seen below. *C.L. Caddy*

Barnham station signal box, built in 1911 to replace the original box when the branch line was doubled. Two electric sets are parked in the sidings to the south of the Bognor line. *Lens of Sutton*

An unusual visitor to Bognor was this Bulleid/Roworth Co-Co mixed traffic electric locomotive seen on the left in this post-war view.   *Lens of Sutton*

Barnham station in 1963, looking down the main line towards Brighton. The Bognor Regis platform can just be seen to the right.   *C.L. Caddy*

London, as in those days most people worked a half day on Saturdays and could not get away for the week-end until after lunch.

The West Sussex timetable as a whole was very complex and required the traveller's close attention; there were notes such as "calls on the first Wednesday of the month to set down London passengers only".

In 1933 there were alterations to the timetables, as many of the local trains on the coast line were terminated at West Worthing to connect with the new electric shuttle trains from there to Brighton.

In February 1936 the Chairman of the Southern Railway, Mr Holland-Martin, announced that both the main Portsmouth lines would be electrified, as well as the Littlehampton and Bognor branches. Work was to be completed by July 1938. The branch lines were the last to be dealt with and so in 1938 work began at Bognor and Barnham. The engine shed at Littlehampton was closed in September 1937 and the workings were transfered to the Bognor shed.

A new 66 lever signal box was built at Bognor in the then popular Odeon style, being sited just south of Bersted Crossing. The old Bersted Crossing and Station signal boxes were then closed and demolished. A fourth platform was added to Bognor Station by converting the old down side cattle dock siding to hold a four car electric set. Platforms one to three were extended to 820 feet to take 12 car rakes. Three carriage sidings were constructed to the east of the up main line; narrow concrete platforms between the sidings enabled easy access for carriage cleaners.

At Barnham Station the 1864 buildings were swept away and a new building erected beside Station Road with a covered walk-way from road level up to the platform. A subway was constructed between the two platforms with access to this walk-way. The island platform was lengthened so that 8 car sets could use the Bognor bay. At the same time facing connections were provided for down trains and the carriage sidings next to the Bognor bay were electrified.

Test runs of the new electric stock were made in May 1938, and one or two party trains of electric stock ran from London Bridge to Bognor during June. On 30th June there was an inaugural ceremony; a train of the new stock with two buffet cars ran from London to Bognor (via Littlehampton), carrying a large party of notables and company officials, augmented at Littlehampton by the Chairman and Clerk of the UDC. The Chairman of Bognor Regis UDC met the train and presided at a luncheon at the Pavilion, at which His Grace the Duke of Norfolk spoke, as did the Southern Railway Chairman and the General Manager. From 3rd July the full electric service commenced; Bognor lost its Pullman services from that date but they were replaced by new electric buffet cars of startling interior design.

During World War II train frequencies to Bognor were reduced and refreshment cars were included in only four trains per day. In 1941 Bognor's engine shed became a sub depot of Horsham although engines were still stabled there.

At the conclusion of the war, as was the situation in 1919, the railways were in a bad way and the Government's solution was the wholesale nationalisation of the railway system. And so from 1st January, 1948 the

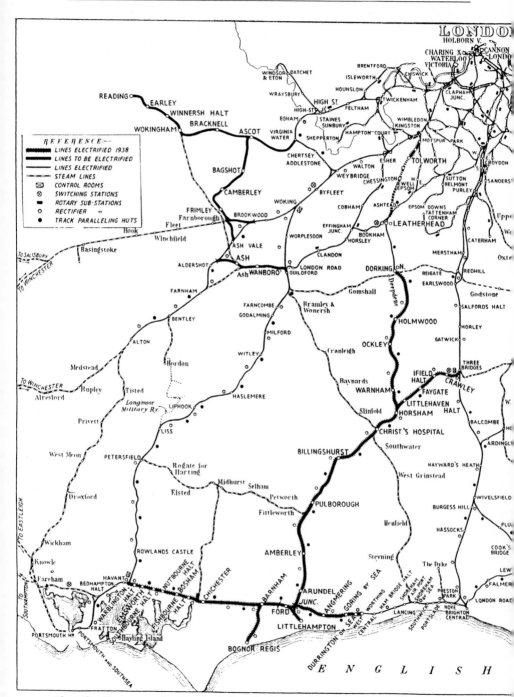

Electrification proposals, 1938 including the Bognor Branch. *Courtesy, Railway Gazette*

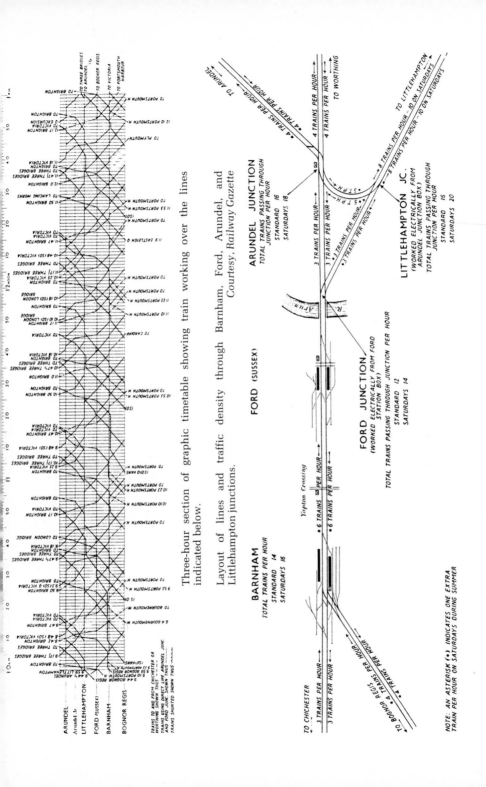

Three-hour section of graphic timetable showing train working over the lines indicated below.

Layout of lines and traffic density through Barnham, Ford, Arundel, and Littlehampton junctions.

Courtesy, Railway Gazette

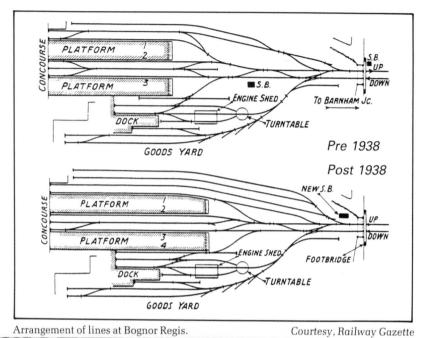

Pre 1938

Post 1938

Arrangement of lines at Bognor Regis.   Courtesy, *Railway Gazette*

The concourse at Bognor station shortly after its opening to the general public in 1901. This view shows the unusual bow front and cupola on the refreshment room.
Oakwood Press Collection

Bognor branch line became part of the Central Section, Southern Region of British Railways. Little changed on the line for the first few years, but in 1953 Bognor engine shed was closed and in 1956 it was mostly demolished, only the south end wall and the offices remaining. The turntable was also removed in 1956 but the pit was not filled in until the early 1960s. Visiting engines did continue to be stabled overnight in the yard up until 1958 when it was handed over to the traffic department. At the same time as the engine shed was closed most of the sidings were also lifted. Olby's built an extension to their wharf on the site for use as a timber store and the old store was converted to a timber mill.

By the 1950s the extra Saturday trains were much reduced as most people were now coming to Bognor by car; in 1956 only one was provided. Saturday Buffet Car services were also much reduced, from the nine on weekdays to five on Saturdays. Another feature of these times was the greater use of cross-country services, which benefited Bognor. Four trains each way between Cardiff and Portsmouth or Brighton gave easy travelling to many places such as Bath and Salisbury. The 8.28 am from Bognor could, by a change at Southampton, bring one to Birmingham in under six hours, no faster than going via London but needing less effort. Railway enthusiasts at this time savoured the experience of riding behind a "West Country" Pacific on what was otherwise an electric line as they also could on the Saturday Brighton–Exeter trains.

The buffet cars had now been downgraded to refreshment cars, but there were more of them. Another nice touch was the extension of the late Pullman train, 10.25 pm from Victoria to Littlehampton, by a connection from there arriving at Bognor at 12.48 am – a great boon to anyone missing the last through train to Bognor which left Victoria at 9.18 pm.

A useful "shot in the arm" came as a result of the opening of Butlin's holiday camp in 1960. Butlin's Camp was built on the Brooklands, south of Hotham Park, on the site of what could have been Bognor railway station if the scheme of 1846 had come to fruition.

By the seventies the late train from London had ceased, but there were more refreshment car trains. The one extra summer train, leaving Victoria at 10.32 am, reached Bognor in 1 hr 28 mins, faster than any other train, by omitting the customary stops at Pullborough and Arundel. The up summer train, however, leaving Bognor at 10.27 am took 14 minutes longer with one stop only (at Sutton) between Barnham and Victoria. Up fast trains were all booked to take about six minutes longer than their down counterparts.

On 3rd May, 1971 the goods facility was closed and the track was subsequently lifted.

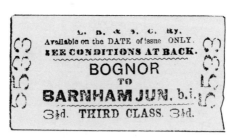

LONDON AND BOGNOR SERVICES—WEEK-DAYS.

7.48 a.m. Bognor to London B.	8 a.m. from London Bridge previously.	London B.	5.8 p.m. from London Bridge	5.8 p.m. London Bridge	W. Worthing and Bognor.	7.18 a.m. from Bognor.
Bogr. 3rd Bk. Bogr. Compo. 2nd & 3rd Bogr. 1st Bogr. 1st Bogr. 1st Bogr. 2nd Bk. Pullman Car Bogr. Compo. 1st & 2nd 1 2nd } M.O. 1 3rd }				Bogr. 3rd Brakes Bogr. Compo. 2 & 3 3 Bogr. Firsts Bogr. Compo. 1 2nd Bk. Pullman Car 1 1st. 1 Bogr. Compo. 1 Tri-Compo. 2 3rd Brakes	Horley.	9. 0 a.m. from Tunbridge Wells.

Extract from the Working Appendix showing the formation of the main line and suburban trains for July 1908.

The Branch timetable for July 1912.

BARNHAM JUNCTION & BOGNOR.

WEEK DAYS.

DOWN.

SUNDAYS.

WEEK DAYS.

UP.

WEEK DAYS—contd.

DOWN.

WEEK DAYS—contd.

UP.

SUNDAYS.

B Commencing July 19th. NS Not Saturdays.

O Not after July 18th.   D June only.   E Commencing July.
Th. O Thursdays only.   ¶ Motor, Third class only.

175

LITTLEHAMPTON TO BARNHAM JUNCTION.—*On Mondays*, if necessary, a Truck of Live Stock for Barnham Market may be sent from Littlehampton to Ford by the 7.25 a.m. Passenger Train, to be attached at latter Station to the 7.50 a.m. Cattle Train from Brighton which must be stopped by Signal at Ford Junction to take the Truck forward. This Truck must be attached behind the rear Brake Van of the 7.25 a.m. Train from Littlehampton, and an extra Brake Van must be run at the rear of the Truck, and a Guard must ride in each Brake Van. (T.T. 17,096.)

BOGNOR BRANCH.

DOWN. — Week Days

		Gds.		M	G		C	M		M	Com. July 13.	Tds.		Not after July 13.	Com. Jly.19.	Not after July 13.
Barnham Jc. dep.		6 40	8 6	8 53	9 30	9 50	9 57	1020	1040	1120	12 5	12 31	1246	1 28	1 40	2 11	2 30	2 43
Bognor arr.		6 55	8 13	9 0	9 40		9 57	10 5	1027	1047	1127	1212	12 38	1253	1 35	1 47	2 18	2 37	2 50

	June only.	July, Aug., Sept.	M		M	SO	M				F	M		M		M	Ety. Motr.
Barnham Jc. dep.	3 13	3 29	3 45	4 20	4 30	4 55	5 30	5 0	6 25	657	7 5	7 35	8 3	8 21	9 45	9 58	1013	11 18
Bognor arr.	3 20	3 36	3 52	4 27	4 38	5 2	5 37	6 7	6 32	7 5	7 12	7 42	8 11	8 28	9 52	10 5	1020	11 25

UP. — Week Days.

		Eng. H		J		M	B	M		D			M	noon	M	Ety. Not after July 13.		Com. July 19th.	Not after Jly.18
Bognor dep.	6 25	7 2	7 48	8 50	9 16	9 35	10 0	10 12	10 5	11 50	12 0	1 20	1 28	1 55	2 5	2 23	
Barnham Jc. arr.	6 32	7 27	7 55	8 37	9 17	9 42	10 7	10 19	10 57	11 57	12 7	1 27	1 35	2 2	2 12	2 30	

	June only.	July, Aug., Sept.	June Gds.	Com. 19th.	July, Aug. and Sept.	June only.		M		M		M			M	M		M		M	Mtr.
Bognor dep.	2 55	2 55	3 5	3 10	3 18	3 30	3 4	40	5 30	5 43	6 40	7 0	7 13	7 43	8 3	9 28	9 45	10 0	10 35
Barnham Jc. arr.	3 2	3 3	3 13	3 18	3 25	3 37	4 10	4 47	5 37	5 50	6 47	7 6	7 20	7 50	8 10	9 35	9 52	10 7	10 42

DOWN. — Sundays.

		Gds.		Gds.				Q	N	Ety.		June only.						
Barnham Jc. dep.	7 5	8 0	9 10	10 8	10 43	10 58	11 12	1132		3 20	4 8	6 18	7 0	8 25	8 52	9 18	1015	
Bognor arr.	7 15	8 7	9 20	10 15	10 50	11 5	11 20	1139		3 27	4 55	6 25	7 7	8 32	8 59	9 25	1022	

UP. — Sundays.

			Q Eng.					Q	July, Aug., Sept.	June only.							
Bognor dep.	6 45	7 35	8 55	9 45	10 20	3 5	4 15	5 54	6 5	6 23	6 32	6 43	3 0	8 37	9 3	9 45	
Barnham Jc. arr.	6 52	7 42	9 2	9 52	10 27	3 12	4 22	6 1	6 12	6 30	6 39	6 50	3 7	8 44	9 10	9 52	

Through Carriages for London Bridge will be run in this Train, which must be attached to the 8.42 a.m. Up Train from Portsmouth Harbour.   **C** 9.0 a.m. Motor ex Brighton.   **D** Motor to Brighton.   **F** Through Train from London Bridge.   **G** Mixed Passenger and Goods when necessary.   **H** Not on Mondays.   Calls at Bersted Crossing to take up Mail Bag for Barnham Junction.   Porter will be in charge of Mail Bag.   **K** When necessary with important Goods loaded after 3.0 p.m.   **J** Through Train to London Bridge.   **M** Motor.   **Q** When necessary.   **SO** Saturdays only.   § With Through Coaches off 8.55 a.m. ex Victoria.

Working timetable for the Branch, September 1912.

BOGNOR & LITTLEHAMPTON TO LONDON.

WEEK DAYS.

UP.	B	B CP Mon Not only Mon	C	O	Thro' Train	O	J	C	B
	a.m	a.m. a.m.	a.m. a.m. a.m.	a.m. a.m. a.m.	p.m. p.m.	p.m.	p.m.	p.m. p.m. p.m.	p.m. p.m. p.m.
BOGNOR ......dep.	...	7 10 7 18 7 18	8 10 8 30 9 10	8 30 9 10 10	12 25	2 0	3 15 ...	5 30 5 37	5 0 9 28 ...
LITTL'HTON dep.	540	6 45 7 10 7 10 7 35	8 15 8 44 9 15 10	11 8 42 12 12 25	2 2	2 52 3 23	3 54	3 55 3 05 5 08	3 08 3 9 48 ...
Sutton arr.		9 h 2	... 9 56 ...	10 22 ...	2 48 3 38 4	...	6 49 7 1	9 34 ...	...
L'NDON B'DGE. ,,	819	9 10	9 58 10 45 10 55	10 45 10 55 12 8	3 32 4 15 4 27	...	7 48 10 8	12 59	...
Clapham Jct. arr.		9 31 ... ... 9 22 10 28	... 10 41	10 41 ...	3 22 ...	4 26 4 52 ...	7 17 7 31 9 53	12 50	...
VICTORIA		9 19 9 29 22 10 28	10 52	11 2 0 3 32	...	4 345 06 507	157 39 10 11 0		

B Via Brighton.   **O** Through Train from Bognor.
  Breakfast Cars run in this train from Bognor.
J Change at Pulboro' and Horsham.
S Slips London Bridge Carriages.

SUNDAYS.

	B	B	B	B	Thro' Train	B
	a.m.	a.m.	a.m.	p.m.	p.m.	p.m. p.m.
	7 25	9 45	10 50	4 15	6 6	6 30 8 0 ...
	7 45	9 55	... 4 5	6	6 0	6 40 7 55
	12 h 21	...	...	7 22	8 15	8 50 11 34
	10 45	...	...	7		...
	12 23	12 49	...	7 41	8 33	10 46 ...
	10 32	0	1 35	7 0	7 49	8 42 10 55

P First and Third Class Pullman
h Change at Horsham.

The October 1922 Branch passenger service.

Southern Railway passenger timetable for July 1923.

BARNHAM JUNCTION & BOGNOR

WEEK DAYS.

DOWN.

	a.m.	a.m. a.m.	a.m. a.m. a.m.	a.m. a.m.	a.m. a.m. a.m.	a.m.	p.m.	p.m. p.m.	p.m. p.m. p.m.	p.m.
BARNHAM JUNC......dep.	7 34	8 5 8 56	9 10 9 25 9 54	10	2 10 28 10 40	11 18	12 30	1 25 2	2 45	3 50 4 32
BOGNOR ....arr.	7 41	8 12 9 3	9 20 9 32 10 1	10	10 35 10 47	11 25 12 37		1 32 2	9 25 2	3 57 4 39

SUNDAYS, CHRISTMAS DAY AND GOOD FRIDAY.

	a.m.	a.m. a.m.	a.m.	p.m. p.m.	p.m. p.m.	p.m.	p.m.	p.m.
BARNHAM JUNC......dep.	7 52	10 8 10 34	10 45 11 12	12 45	1 0 2 5	3 15 4 45	30 5 0 6	7 4 ...
BOGNOR	7 59	10 15 10 41	10 52 11 19	12 52	1 7 2 12	3 22 4 51	37 5 7 6	7 11 ...

UP.

WEEK DAYS.

	p.m. Sats only.	a.m. a.m. a.m.	a.m. a.m. a.m.	a.m. a.m.	a.m. a.m.	a.m.	p.m.	p.m.	p.m. p.m.	p.m. p.m.	p.m.
BOGNOR ....dep.	7 59	8 12 7 46 8 10	8 30 9 10 9 37	10 00 10 55	11 12 11 45	12 12	1 0 1 21	2 0 3	3 15 3 25 4 15	4 45 30 5	6 15 6 45 7 20 7 50
BARNHAM JUNC. .....arr.	8 6	8 19 7 53 8 17	8 37 9 17 9 44	10 07 11 0	11 19 11 52	12 19	1 7	2 12 2 27	3 22 3 32 4 24	51 4	5 37 6 22 7 27 7 57

SUNDAYS, CHRISTMAS DAY AND GOOD FRIDAY.

	a.m.	a.m.	a.m. a.m.	a.m.	p.m.	p.m.	p.m.	p.m.	p.m.	p.m.
BOGNOR ....dep.	9 28	10 10	6 40 7 25 9 45	10 20 10 50	4 15	6 30	6 44	8 0	9 10 5	
BARNHAM JUNC.	9 35	10 17	6 47 7 52 9 52	10 27 10 57	4 22	6 37	6 51	8 7	9 17 0 5	

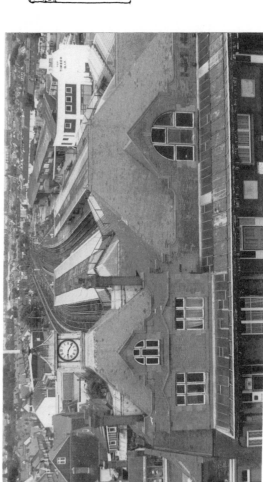

This view of Bognor station taken from a precarious position on the roof of Reynolds depository shows the station layout today. Only the platforms and carriage sidings are still served by rails, the old goods yard is a car park for Olby's DIY Merchants and the coal sidings are now waste ground.

Author

BOGNOR REGIS and BARNHAM.

Up. — Week Days.

	Miles		mrn	mrn	mrn	mrn	mrn	mrn	mrn	mrn	mrn	mrn	mrn	mrn	mrn	mrn	mrn	mrn	mrn	mrn		aft	aft	aft
Bognor Regis		dep.	5 15	530	6 30	7 8	715	7 34	8 9	8 32	9 0	9 35	9 52	1010	1036	1038	..	1052	1112	1135	1152	..	12 6	1228	1237
Barnham 250, 258	3¼	arr.	5 22	537	637	715	721	7 41	8 16	8 39	9 7	9 42	9 59	1017	1043	1045	..	10 9	1119	1142	1159	..	1213	1235	1244

Up. — Week Days—Continued.

		aft	aft	aft	aft	aft	aft		aft	aft	aft	aft	aft	aft		aft	aft	aft	aft	aft		aft
Bognor Regis	dep.	1255	1 3	153	2 0	2 42	2 40	..	3 20	3 53	4 20	4 33	4 52	5 10	5 20	..	5 40	5 50	5 59	6 46	7 13	..	7 42
Barnham 250, 258	arr.	1 3	110	2 0	2 7	2 31	2 47	..	3 27	4 0	4 27	4 40	4 59	5 17	5 27	..	5 47	5 57	6 6	6 53	7 20	..	7 49

Up. — Week Days—Continued.   **Sundays.**

		aft	aft	aft	aft	aft	aft	aft	W SO	mn	mn	mn	mn	mn		mrn	mrn	mrn	mrn		aft
Bognor Regis	dep.	7 50	8	8 30	8 53	9 18	9 39	9 56	10 4	1045	11 10	640	720	754	854	9 40	955	..	1035	11 6	1129	1152	..	1213
Barnham 250, 258	arr.	7 57	8 15	8 37	9 5	9 25	9 46	10 3	1011	1052	11 17	647	727	8 1	9 1	9 47	102	..	1042	1113	1136	1159	..	1220

Up. — Sundays—Continued.

		aft		aft		aft		aft	aft		aft	aft	aft	aft		aft	aft	aft	aft
Bognor Regis	dep.	1258	..	150	..	230	..	259	..	355	4 34	432	453	..	5 4	355	..	642	658	750	812	..	855	943	1010	1020	..
Barnham 250, 258	arr.	1 5	..	2 6	..	237	..	3 6	..	4 2	410	439	5 0	..	5 506	2	..	649	7 7	757	819	..	9 5	950	1017	1027	..

8 O Sats. only.   **8 X** Sats. excepted.   **W 8 O** Weds. and Sats. only.

BARNHAM and BOGNOR REGIS.

Down. — Week Days.

	Miles		mrn	mrn	mrn	mrn	mrn	mrn		mn	mn	mn	mrn	S X		mrn	8 O	mrn		mrn	mrn		aft	aft	aft	aft
Barnham		dep	617	642	722	752	822	850	..	923	933	954	10 8	1023	..	1056	11 4	1119	..	1126	1150	..	1228	1235	1245	1 16
Bognor Regis	3¼	arr.	625	649	729	759	829	857	..	930	940	101	1016	1031	..	11 3	1111	1127	..	1135	1157	..	1235	1242	1250	1 23

Down. — Week Days—Continued.

		aft	aft	aft	aft	8 O	8 X	8 O	aft	aft	aft	aft	aft	aft	aft	aft	8 O	8 X	aft	aft	aft	aft
Barnham	dep	1 22	1 57	2 20	2 43	3 17	3 18	3 22	5 43	419	447	5 5	5 18	5 27	5 41	6 36	126	287	0 7	2 7	247	3 17	4 68	8 0
Bognor Regis	arr.	1 30	2 5	2 27	2 50	3 24	3 26	3 30	3 50	427	454	5 13	5 265	35	5 48	610	6 20	6 367	8 7	107	317	367	548	8 7

Down. — Week Days—Continued.   **Sundays.**

		aft	aft	aft	aft	aft	aft	aft	aft	aft	W SO	mn	mn	mn	mn	mn		mrn	mrn	mrn	mrn		aft	aft
Barnham	dep	8 20	8 43	9 12	9 19	9 31	956	1016	1023	1056	11 20	127	5 728	4 9	9101	10 8	11 2	1119	1126	1150	..	1218	1235
Bognor Regis	arr.	8 27	8 50	9 19	9 26	9 38	103	1023	1031	11 3	1127	12 33	7128	4 9	9101	10 8	11 2	1119	1126	1150	..	1226	1242

Down. — Sundays—Continued.

		aft	aft		aft		aft		aft	aft		aft	aft		aft	aft	aft	aft		aft	aft		aft
Barnham	dep	1 17	213	..	234	..	313	..	413	421	..	444	513	..	611	630	..	713	813	8 51	919	..	10 0	1022	1036	..	1117
Bognor Regis	arr.	1 25	220	..	241	..	320	..	420	428	..	451	520	..	619	637	..	720	820	8 59	927	..	10 7	1030	1043	..	1125

8 O Saturdays only.   **8 X** Saturdays excepted.   **W 8 O** Wednesdays and Saturdays.

Bradshaw's timetable for 1938.

BOGNOR REGIS, LITTLEHAMPTON, ARUNDEL & LONDON

UP — WEEK DAYS	SO am	RB am	SX RB am	SO RB am	SO P am	SX P am	SO am	SX P am	SO am	SX RB am	SO RB am	SX P am	SO P am	SX am	SO am	SX RB am		am	RB am
BOGNOR REGIS ... dep	6 22	..	7 4	7 6	..	..	..	7 20	7 20	7 52	8 0	..	..	8 4	8 6	8 27	..	8 36	9A 0
Littlehampton ... "	6 42	6 39	7 7	....	7 8	7 21	7 25	7 37	7 43	7 59	8 4	8 8	8 8	8 22	8 25	....	....	8 55	....
Arundel ... "	6 48	..	7 18	7 21	..	..	7 32	..	7 51	8 9	8 18	..	..	8 29	8 32	8 41	..	9 2	9 18
LONDON London Bridge ... arr	8*26	8 26	8*43	....	....	9 10	....	9 22	9 22	9*32	....	9 51	....	....	....	9 58	....	....	....
" Victoria ... "	8 22	..	8 34	8 44	8 57	9*15	9 15	9 20	..	9 31	9 40	..	9 57	10 18	10 15	..	..	10 48	10 40

UP — WEEK DAYS—continued	P am	am	am	RB am	P am		am	am	RB am	am	SO RB am	am	SO RB noon	P pm		pm	pm	SO RB pm	P pm
BOGNOR REGIS ... dep	..	9 6	9 36	10A 0	..	..	10 6	10 36	11A 0	11 6	11 30	11 36	12A 0	..	..	12 6	12 36	1A 0	..
Littlehampton ... "	9A 8	9 25	9 55	....	10A 8	....	10 25	10 55	....	11 25	....	11 55	....	12A 8	....	12 25	12 55	....	1A 8
Arundel ... "	..	9 32	10 2	10 18	..	..	10 32	11 2	11 18	11 32	..	12 2	12 18	..	..	12 32	1 2	1 18	..
LONDON London Bridge ... arr	....	....	....	....	....	....	....	....	....	....	....	....	....	....	....	....	....	....	....
" Victoria ... "	10 55	11 15	11 45	11 j40	11 57	..	12 15	12 45	12 j40	1 15	1 12	1 45	1 40	1 55	..	2 15	2 45	2 40	2655

UP — WEEK DAYS—continued	pm	pm	SO RB pm	SX RB pm	P pm	pm	SO pm	SX pm	SO pm	RB pm	SO P pm		pm	SO pm	SX pm	RB pm	SX pm	SO pm	pm	RB pm
BOGNOR REGIS ... dep	1 6	1 36	2A 0	2A 0	..	2 6	..	2 36	2 36	3A†0	..	..	3 6	3 36	3 36	4A 0	4 6	4 10	4 40	5A 0
Littlehampton ... "	1 25	1 55	....	....	2A 8	2 25	....	2 55	2 55	....	3A 8	....	3 25	3 55	3 55	....	4 25	4 29	4 59	....
Arundel ... "	1 32	2 2	2 18	2 18	..	2 32	2 48	3 2	3 2	3 18	..	..	3 32	4 2	4 2	4 18	4 32	4 35	5 6	5 18
LONDON London Bridge ... arr	....	....	....	....	....	....	....	....	....	....	....	....	....	....	....	....	....	....	....	....
" Victoria ... "	3615	3645	3H45	3 40	3 55	4 15	4 17	4 53	4 45	4 40	4 55	..	5 16	5 45	5 58	5 j40	6 15	6 15	6 j45	6 40

UP — WEEK DAYS—continued	SX P pm	SO pm	SO pm		pm	pm	SO pm	SO pm	SO pm	SX pm	SO pm	SX pm	SX P pm	SO pm	SX pm	pm	pm	pm	pm	pm
BOGNOR REGIS ... dep	..	..	5 6	..	5 40	6A 0	..	6 6	6 36	6 37	7A 0	7A 0	..	..	..	7 36	8A 0	..	8 45	10 27
Littlehampton ... "	5A 2	5A 8	5 25	....	5 59	....	6A 8	6 25	6 55	6 59	....	....	7A 8	7A 8	7 26	7 55	....	8A 8	9 9	10 35
Arundel ... "	..	..	5 32	..	6 6	6 18	..	6 32	7 2	7 5	7 18	7 18	..	..	7 33	8 2	8 18	..	9 16	10 47
LONDON Victoria ... arr	6 57	6 55	7 15	....	7 45	7 40	7 55	8 15	8 45	8 45	8 40	8 40	8 55	8 55	9 15	9 45	9 40	9 55	10 50	12 17

UP — SUNDAYS	am	am	am	RB am	P am	am	am	am	am	pm	pm	pm	pm	pm	pm	P pm	pm	RB pm	pm
BOGNOR REGIS ... dep	6 36	7 36	8 36	9A 0	..	9 36	10A 0	10 36	11 36	12 6	12 36	1 6	1 36	2 6	2 36	..	3 36	4A 0	4 40
Littlehampton ... "	6 55	7 55	8 55	8 55	9A 8	9 55	9 55	10 55	11 55	12 25	12 55	1 25	1 55	2 25	2 55	3A 8	3 55	3 55	4 59
Arundel ... "	7 2	8 2	9 2	9 18	..	10 2	10 18	11 2	12 2	12 32	1 2	1 32	2 2	2 32	3 2	..	4 2	4 18	5 6
LONDON Victoria arr	8 45	9 45	10 45	10 40	10 55	11 45	11 40	12 45	1 45	2 15	2 45	3 15	3 45	4 15	4 45	4 55	5 45	5 40	6 45

UP — SUNDAYS—continued	P pm	pm	pm	pm	pm		pm	pm	pm	pm	pm		pm	pm		pm	pm	pm	pm
BOGNOR REGIS ... dep	..	5 6	5 36	6A 0	..	..	6 6	6 36	7 0	..	7 15	..	7 36	8 0	..	..	8 36	9 0	9 45
Littlehampton ... "	5A 8	5 30	5 55	5 55	6A 8	....	6 25	6 55	6 55	7A 8	7 35	....	7 55	7 55	....	8 8	8 55	8 55	10 9
Arundel ... "	..	..	6 2	6 18	..	..	..	7 2	7 18	..	..	..	8 2	8 18	..	..	9 2	9 18	10 16
LONDON Victoria arr	6 55	7 15	7 45	7 43	7 55	....	8 15	8 49	8 43	8 57	9 15	....	9 45	9 43	....	9 55	10 45	10 40	11 52

A Seats may be reserved at a fee of 2/- per seat, upon personal or postal request to the Station Master. Early application is advisable
6 2 minutes later on Saturdays
g 3 minutes later on Saturdays
j 2 minutes later on Mondays to Fridays

H 5 minutes *earlier* 23rd June and 8th September
P Includes limited Pullman Car facilities, for supplementary fees and further information, see pages 24 and 61
RB Buffet Car

SO Saturdays only
SX Mondays to Fridays

* Change at East Croydon
† Seats may be reserved on Saturdays only

HEAVY FIGURES INDICATE THROUGH CARRIAGES TO LONDON

Summary of Principal Services—continued
For full service—see Table 28

LONDON & ARUNDEL, LITTLEHAMPTON & BOGNOR REGIS

DOWN — WEEK DAYS	SX am	SO am	SX am	SO am	SO am	am	am	SX RB am	SO RB am	P am	am	SO RB am	am	SX RB am	SO RB am	P am	am	SO RB am
LONDON Victoria ... dep	7 1	7 6	7 59	8 6	8 18	8g33	9H 2	9A18	9A21	9A25	9g33	9A48	10H 2	10A18	10A21	10A25	10 36	10A48
" London Bridge ... "	....	....	....	....	....	....	....	....	....	....	....	....	....	....	....	....	....	....
Arundel ... arr	8 36	8 46	9 36	9 46	9 38	10 17	10 46	10 38	10 59	..	11 17	11 8	11 46	11 38	12 2	..	12 17	12 7
Littlehampton ... "	8 43	8 53	9 43	9 53	9 53	10 25	10 53	10 53	....	11H10	11 24	....	11 53	11 53	....	12614	12 24	....
BOGNOR REGIS ... "	9 7	9 13	10 7	10 13	9 54	10 43	11 13	10 54	11 19	..	11 43	11 25	12 13	11 54	12 19	..	12 43	12 25

DOWN — WEEK DAYS—continued	am	SX RB am	SO RB am	P am	am	SO am	pm	RB pm		SO P pm	pm	pm	SO RB pm	SO pm	pm	pm	RB pm
LONDON Victoria ... dep	11 6	11A18	11A21	11A25	11 36	11 48	12 6	12A‡18	..	12 25	12 36	1 6	1A18	1 25	1 36	2 6	2A18
" London Bridge ... "	....	....	....	....	....	....	....	....	....	12*14	....	....	....	....	....	....	....
Arundel ... arr	12 46	12 38	12 59	..	1 17	1 7	1 46	1 38	..	..	2 17	2 46	2 38	..	3 17	3 46	3 38
Littlehampton ... "	12 53	12 53	....	1E10	1 24	....	1 53	1 53	....	2 12	2 24	2 53	2 53	3 14	3 24	3 53	3 53
BOGNOR REGIS ... "	1 13	12 54	1 19	..	1 43	1 25	2 13	1 54	..	..	2 43	3 13	2 54	..	3 43	4 13	3 54

DOWN — WEEK DAYS—continued	P pm	pm	pm	RB pm	P pm	pm	pm	RB pm	P pm	SX pm	SO pm	SO pm	SX RB pm	SX RB pm	SX RB pm	SO RB pm	SO P pm
LONDON Victoria ... dep	2A25	2 36	3 6	3A18	3A25	3 36	4 6	4A18	4A25	4 33	4 36	5 6	..	5 2	5 2	5A18	5A25
" London Bridge ... "	....	....	....	....	....	....	....	....	....	....	....	....	5 5	5 14	....	....	....
Arundel ... arr	..	4h17	4 46	4 38	..	5 17	5 46	5 38	..	6 10	6 17	6 46	..	6 34	6 45	6 38	..
Littlehampton ... "	4H10	4h24	4 53	4 53	5H10	5 24	5 53	5 53	6 10	6 19	6 24	6 53	6 46	6 52	6 52	....	7 10
BOGNOR REGIS ... "	..	4h43	5 13	4 54	..	5 43	6 13	5 54	..	..	6 43	7 13	..	6 51	..	6 54	..

DOWN — WEEK DAYS—continued	SX RB pm	SX P pm	SO pm	SX pm	SX pm	SO pm	SX RB pm	SX RB pm	SO RB pm	SX P pm	SX pm	SO pm	RB pm	PX pm	pm	pm	pm	P pm
LONDON Victoria ... dep	5 29	5 34	5 36	..	..	6 2	..	6 18	6A18	6 33	7 2	7 6	7A18	7A25	8 6	9A18	9 36	10 45
" London Bridge ... "	....	....	....	5 43	5 47	....	6 4	....	....	....	....	....	....	....	....	....	....	....
Arundel ... arr	6 49	..	7 17	..	7 16	7 36	..	7 31	7 38	..	8 46	8 46	8 38	..	9 46	10 38	11 17	..
Littlehampton ... "	7 9	7 18	7 24	7 26	....	7 43	7 46	7 49	....	8 18	8 53	8 53	8 53	9 10	9 53	11 7	11 24	12 30
BOGNOR REGIS ... "	7 3	..	7 43	..	7 33	8 7	..	7 47	7 54	..	9 13	9 13	8 54	....	10 13	10 56	11 43	12 47

DOWN — SUNDAYS	am	am	am	am		am	P am		am	am	am	am	am	am	RB am	P am	am	pm	pm	pm
LONDON Victoria dep	7 6	8 6	8 36	9 6	..	9A21	9A25	..	9 36	10 6	10A18	10A25	10 36	11 6	11A18	11A25	11 36	12 6	12 36	1 6
Arundel ... arr	8 46	9 46	....	10 46	....	10 59	....	....	....	11 46	11 38	....	....	12 46	12 38	....	....	1 46	....	2 46
Littlehampton ... "	8 53	9 53	10 18	10 53	..	..	11 10	..	11 18	11 53	11 53	12 14	12 18	12 53	12 53	1 10	1 18	1 53	2 18	2 53
BOGNOR REGIS ... "	9 13	10 13	10 37	11 13	....	11 19	....	....	11 39	12 13	11 54	....	12 41	1 13	12 54	....	1 41	2 13	2 41	3 13

DOWN — SUNDAYS—continued	pm	pm	pm	pm		pm	pm	pm	P pm	pm	pm	pm	RB pm	P pm	pm	pm	pm	pm	pm	pm
LONDON Victoria dep	2 6	2A25	3 6	3A18	..	4 6	4 36	5 6	5A25	5 36	6 6	7 6	7A18	7A25	8 6	8 25	9 6	9 18	9 25	10 18
Arundel ... arr	3 46	....	4 46	4 41	....	5 46	6 17	6 46	....	7 17	7 46	8 46	8 41	....	9 46	....	10 46	10 44	....	....
Littlehampton ... "	3 53	4 10	4 53	4 53	..	5 53	6 24	6 53	7 10	7 24	7 53	8 53	8 53	9 11	9 53	10 10	10 53	10 53	11 10	..
BOGNOR REGIS ... "	4 13	....	5 13	4 58	....	6 13	6 43	7 13	....	7 43	8 13	9 13	8 58	....	10 13	....	11 13	10 56	....	11 50

A Seats may be reserved at a fee of 2/- per seat, upon personal or postal request to the station Master. Early application is advisable
E 6 minutes later on Saturdays
e 7 minutes later on Saturdays
6 2 minutes later on Saturdays
g 3 minutes later on Saturdays
H 4 minutes later on Saturdays
h 5 minutes later on Saturdays

P Includes limited Pullman Car facilities, for supplementary fees and further information, see pages 24 and 61
PX Includes limited Pullman Car facilities on Mondays to Fridays. For supplementary fees and further information, see pages 24 and 61.

RB Buffet Car
SO Saturdays only
SX Mondays to Fridays

* Change at East Croydon
‡ Seats may be reserved on Monday to Friday ONLY

HEAVY FIGURES INDICATE THROUGH CARRIAGES FROM LONDON

The British Rail (Southern Region) timetable for September 1962.

WORTHING (Central), HOVE, BRIGHTON & LONDON

WEEK DAYS

WORTHING (Central) dep
Hove —
Brighton —
LONDON London Bridge arr
  — Victoria —

WEEK DAYS—continued

SUNDAYS

UP

@ Second class only.
† Seats may be reserved on Mondays to Fridays ONLY
▲ Seats may be reserved at fee of 2/- each, and, upon personal or postal request to the Station Master. Early application is advisable.
■ 10 minutes later on Saturdays

PP Pullman Cars only from Brighton, limited accommodation for supplementary fees and further information, see pages 24 and 61
PB Includes limited Pullman Car facilities, see pages 24 and 61
PBX Includes limited Pullman Car facilities on Mondays to Fridays only. For supplementary fees and further information, see pages 24 and 61
PB Pullman Car facilities from Brighton on Mondays to Fridays
RB Buffet Car facilities from Brighton
RBX RB Buffet Car on Mondays to Fridays, SO or Saturdays only
SX Mondays to Fridays

HEAVY FIGURES INDICATE THROUGH CARRIAGES TO LONDON

LONDON & ARUNDEL, LITTLEHAMPTON & BOGNOR REGIS

DOWN

WEEK DAYS

LONDON Victoria dep
  — London Bridge —
Arundel arr
Littlehampton —
BOGNOR REGIS —

WEEK DAYS—continued

SUNDAYS

DOWN

▲ Seats may be reserved at a fee of 2/- each, upon personal or postal request to the Station Master. Early application is advisable.
■ 6 minutes later on Saturdays
● 5 minutes later on Saturdays
● 4 minutes later on Saturdays
■ 3 minutes later on Saturdays
■ 5 minutes later on Saturdays

P Includes limited Pullman Car facilities, for supplementary fees and further information, see pages 24 and 61
PX Includes limited Pullman Car facilities on Mondays to Fridays. For supplementary fees and further information, see pages 24 and 61

RB Buffet Car
SO Saturdays only
SX Mondays to Fridays

* Change at East Croydon. Seats may be reserved on Mondays to Friday ONLY

HEAVY FIGURES INDICATE THROUGH CARRIAGES FROM LONDON

Chapter Seven
The Line and Service Today

Today, remains of the 1902 rebuilding at Bognor still abound. The station house is almost as built except that the large general waiting room is now boarded off and only a small area is left in front of the ticket office, seats are provided in the concourse for waiting passengers. With the exception of the engine shed and station signal box, all the buildings remain, but not in railway use. The goods shed is now a warehouse for Olby's and the large area previously in use for coal sidings is now waste land used for storing building materials. The office block left after the demolition of the engine shed is now a derelict shell and is in danger of collapse.

Several LB&SCR relics on view at the station include a Saxby and Farmer ground frame behind the buffers between platforms 2 and 3, a brace of bench seats on platform 2 and a pair of windows which announce that the parcels office of today was the telegraph office of yesterday. Changes in the road system have made Bersted Crossing redundant and one set of gates have been removed and a wire fence put up in their place but the footbridge remains to enable pedestrians to cross the line. A new road bridge has been built to carry Bognor's new ring road which crosses the line 100 yards north of the old level crossing.

Little remains of the 1864 Barnham Junction except for the buildings on the island platform which are relatively unchanged. The general waiting room still has two original LB&SCR windows.

Other remains of Bognor's railway history are extant at Woodgate Crossing where the original 1846 Woodgate (for Bognor) station and crossing keeper's cottage still stand, although changed slightly in appearance by the addition of extensions by later owners.

Although Bognor still attracts its fair share of tourists and day trippers most of these now come to the town by coach or car, the railway carrying fewer excursionists now than it did even a few years ago.

The town is well within the ever-increasing commuter belt for London and this is reflected in the timetable, which has five departures for Victoria and one London Bridge semi-fast between 6.17 and 8.21 am to cope with the large volume of "City Gents" who travel daily to the Capital. Seats are hard to come by on these rush hour trains, and someone getting on at Bognor very often would hold a seat for a companion getting on further up the line. The author well remembers the times when he has had occasion to get an early train to London and received stony stares and outraged silence when he sat in "old George's" seat, the entire journey being spent facing an unbroken wall of *Guardian* newspapers.

Those working in Brighton or Portsmouth are equally well served, with six early morning trains to Brighton, four of which are made by connecting with Portsmouth Harbour–Brighton Coast Ways services at Barnham, and seven Portsmouth trains using similar Coast Ways/Barnham connections.

The bulk of the daily workload for the Bognor line consists of hourly Victoria semi-fasts at 6 minutes past the hour and hourly Littlehampton and Barnham services at 16 and 40 minutes past the hour. Portsmouth and Brighton are reached by half-hourly Coast Ways services connecting at Barnham.

Both Bognor and Barnham are now resplendent in their new Network South-east liveries of red, white and blue paintwork, a colour scheme which sits well on the old cast iron and woodwork of the stations.

Bognor station on Sunday 4th September, 1988; the 4CIG and 4VEP sets are stabled ready for the Monday morning rush.   *Author*

4VEP set No. 3089 pulls into Barnham station from Bognor Regis on its way to Littlehampton.   *Author*

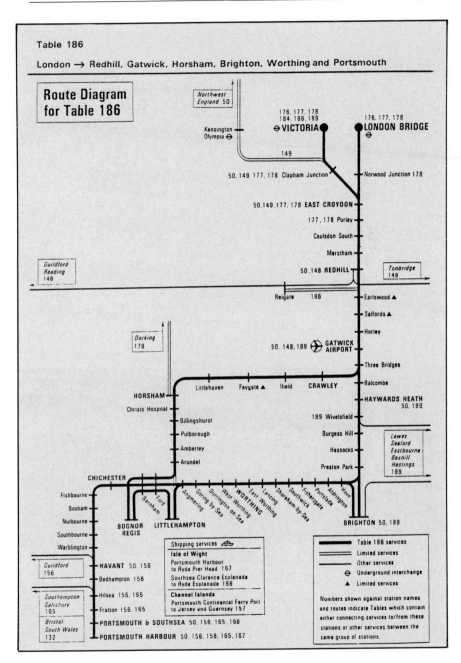

The British Rail 1987–88 Route Diagram including the Bognor Regis Branch.

Ex-branch line engine *Bognor*. Built in 1869 by Kitson and Co. she was numbered 76 by the LB & SCR and as such served on the Bognor branch for several months in 1872. Renumbered 358 in 1877 she ran on the Hayling Island branch. In 1886 she received yet another new number, 496, and ended her days at Littlehampton, being withdrawn in 1895.

Author's Collection

No. 112, an 'E1' class 0−6−0T, propels a typical LB & SCR round-ended open wagon past the locomotive shed at Bognor in February 1927.

R.M. Casserley

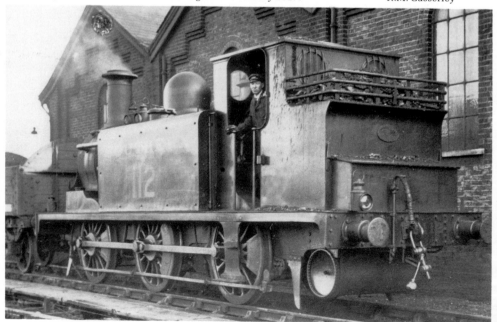

Chapter Eight
Locomotives on the Line

The first locomotive to use the line was an old Sharp, Roberts and Company 2–2–2, No. 29, built in 1845. It only spent a few months on the line, being withdrawn and broken up in November of 1864.

The next two locomotives were both Brighton built 2–2–2s, Nos. 139 and 140. These two engines took turns on the line; both engines were built in 1860 and stayed on the branch until the early 1870s. No. 139 was involved in an unfortunate accident on 12th February, 1869, when during a snow-storm it fell into the turntable pit. The crew claimed that poor visibility caused the accident, however the railway company found them at fault and fined them a day's pay.

In 1872 a small 0–4–2 saddle tank, No. 76, was moved from the Little-hampton branch to work the Bognor line. William Stroudley, the LB&SCR's chief locomotive engineer, had altered the cab and funnel and added spring safety valves to the dome, thus changing the original 1869 design. Named *Bognor* the engine spent only a few months on the line before being sent back to Littlehampton.

Following *Bognor's* short stay on the branch the duties were taken over by 2–2–2 No. 31, renumbered 259 and named *Littlehampton* in May 1876; this loco remained at Bognor until 1878.

After several years of having fairly new engines on the branch line the replacement for *Littlehampton* was a 19-year-old 2–2–2 tank engine, No. 214 named *Seaford*. Stroudley had done his usual modernisation work on the old locomotive and it was mechanically sound, but the boiler tubes gave so much trouble (continually collapsing), that it was withdrawn in September 1879.

In the early 1880s the first of the famous Stroudley 'A1' class "Terriers" to work the line came on the scene; this was No. 38, *Milwall*. This locomotive worked the line until replaced by two more "Terriers". Nos. 45 *Merton* and 78 *Knowle* which took over until 1902 when another of Stroudley's engines, this time a 'D1' class, No. 228 *Seaford* replaced them. *Seaford* had only a short stay because the next year two more "Terriers", No. 77, *Wonersh*, and No. 80 *Bookham* took up the working. These two engines worked the line until the 1911 doubling of the track and opening of the branch line for direct running, when the 'A1s' were displaced by two 'D1' locos fitted for motor-train running.

After World War I the allocation grew with the improved services and by the 1923 grouping there were no fewer than five locomotives of various classes on shed: these were 'D1', No. 259; 'B2x', No. 321; 'I3', No. 75; and 'E1s', Nos. 144 and 150. By 1925 the number of engines had grown to twelve, four 'B4s', two 'B4xs', two 'D1s', one 'E1' and three 'E5s'. In 1930 the allo-cation of 'D1' class engines doubled and Nos. 605, 615, 299 and 616 were on shed.

A Bognor shed 'D1' class roster in 1931 comprised the following: Bognor –Barnham Jn., then to Portsmouth, back to Chichester, up to Dorking North, back to Horsham, six trips between Horsham and Three Bridges, then Hor-

'D1' class No. 2356 stands outside Bognor locomotive shed in this pre-war scene. In front of the 'D1' can be seen the tender of class 'H2' "Atlantic" No. 2425.

Courtesy Historical Model Railway Society

Another 'D1' locomotive, No. 2237, this time waiting for the "right-away" from platform three. In the background is class 'D1' No. 2227.

Courtesy Historical Model Railway Society

Ex-LB & SCR locomotive No. 8, built in 1907 and seen here at Bognor station in pre-war Southern Railway colours.   *Courtesy Historical Model Railway Society*

"Terriers" *Merton* and *Knowle*, the branch line engines from the late 1890s until 1902, seen here at Bognor. The four-wheeled wagon in front of *Knowle* is a Stroudley design horse box.   *Lens of Sutton*

sham to Bognor, a return trip to Barnham Jn., 1½ hours carriage shunting, then a further trip to Barnham and back.

The allocation for 1932 was two 'B4s', five 'H2' "Atlantics", two 'I1s', seven 'D1s', two 'C2xs' and one 'E1'. Next year the allocation had almost completely changed; it was now six 'D1s', four 'H2s', two 'E4s' and one 'C2x'. The reason for the slight drop in numbers was the electrification of the main line to Brighton. Apart from a number of 'D1s' being replaced by 'D3' class engines nothing else changed until 1938 when the Bognor branch was electrified. After electrification the allocation was drastically reduced to only three 'E4' class engines for local goods working. Even this small number was withdrawn in 1941 when the shed became a sub-depot of Horsham.

During 1950 several 'I1x' class engines were in store in Bognor shed along with two of the unfinished "Leader" class locomotives, Nos. 36002/3.

The shed code for locomotives stabled at Bognor, which was painted on the buffer beam, was a rather unflattering "BOG".

The large amount of excursion workings into Bognor meant that many engines not normally seen in the town would come down for a day trip to the coast. In LB & SCR days engines from New Cross Gate and Battersea had a change from the grime of London; the types mainly used were Stroudley singles and the famous 0−4−2 'B1' class "Gladstone's". In the Southern Railway era a few "foreign" engines appeared on the line, these included ex-SE & CR class 'L' 4−4−0s and ex-LSWR 'L12' 4−4−0's. In June 1957 an LMR class '5' 4−6−2 locomotive visited on an excursion from Tring in Herts, a most unusual sight at Bognor.

'B4' class locomotives worked through trains from London to Bognor for 30 years. This is No. 66 *Billinton*, built in 1901 seen here on the turntable at Bognor locomotive shed in 1926.   *R.M. Casserley*

Driver Joe Miller brings in the last regular steam hauled passenger train from Victoria on 2nd July, 1938. The first electric train the next day received a civic reception, but the engine drivers at Bognor were not so happy and hung an effigy on the locomotive shed doors with a card round its neck saying 'To all locomen—R.I.P.'.

Gerard Young Collection

An 'I1x' 4–4–2, No. 2603, brings empty excursion stock from Bognor Regis into Barnham for stabling on 28th March, 1937. *R.W. Kidner*

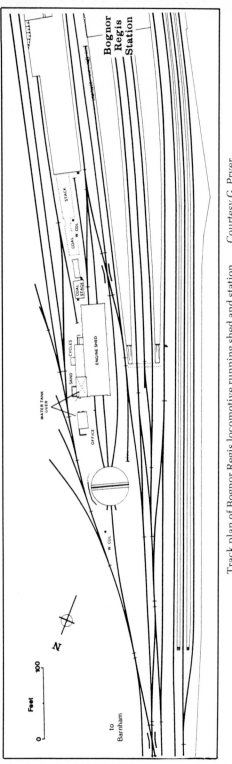

Track plan of Bognor Regis locomotive running shed and station.　　Courtesy G. Pryer

Bognor locomotive running shed before World War II. An 'H2' "Atlantic" No. 2425 is inside the shed while class 'D1' No. 2356 simmers outside.　　H.C. Casserley

'C2' class No. 62433 simmers outside Bognor locomotive shed in this 1954 view, taken from a passing carriage window. *J.E. Kite*

An unusually empty locomotive shed at Bognor in Southern Railway days. The grounded body on the right is an old Stroudley brake third coach. *Lens of Sutton*

4BUF-set No. 3078 having just passed over Bersted crossing on its way to Barnham Junction to join the Portsmouth–Victoria train, 3rd November, 1951.   *E.R. Morten*

Third class auto-trailer No. 1342 involved in a collision at Bognor station in September 1913. It cannot have been too serious as the story did not even make the local papers.   *Lens of Sutton*

Chapter Nine
Coaching Stock used on the Line

Steam Stock

Study of the photographs of the first train at Bognor show that the earliest carriages on the line were old Craven coaches. The make-up of the branch train for a long time was a full brake followed by a 1st, 2nd and 3rd class coach. In the 1880's the ancient Craven stock was replaced by new Stroudley carriages and the normal make up of the train was: full brake, 3rd class, 1st/2nd composite, 1st class, 3rd class and full brake (all Stroudley 4-wheelers). In about 1905 this was replaced by Billinton-designed 6-wheelers.

For the 1911 rail motor services "Balloon" coaches were introduced, so called because of their high, round roofs. The "Balloons" were phased out in the mid-30s and replaced by ex-LSWR two-coach compartment sets which worked the line until electrification.

Through train stock consisted of non-corridor bogie coaches which were replaced by the Southern Railway in 1925. The new 11-coach set, No. 472, was built to an LSWR design known as "Ironclads". In 1929 a new 6-coach set and a 3-coach set of Maunsell design, Nos. 387 and 456 respectively, were introduced. Any new stock after this was acquired from the Brighton and Eastbourne lines as they were electrified, including displaced Pullman cars until they again became redundant following electrification to Bognor in 1938.

During the 1970s there was one loco-hauled service to Bognor, a van train from Havant at 4.50 am on Sundays only; the vans returned on Monday by freight train.

Electric Stock

Following the introduction of the 3rd rail electric system in 1938 the local services were run by 2 BIL sets, except for a short period in 1938 when 2 HAL sets intended for the Eastern Section, were run in on the branch. The 2 BIL sets, numbered 2117–2152 which were built in 1938, lasted on the branch until 1970 when the last set went following a period of gradual withdrawal.

Main line services were operated by 4 COR sets, numbers 3130–3155 and 4 BUF sets containing buffet cars, numbers 3073–3085. Although the electric stock provided in 1937 for the electrification from Waterloo to Portsmouth had included restaurant cars, in this case it was decreed that only buffet cars would be afforded. However these created something of a sensation. Their exterior was unusual in that the bar section had no windows, and the words "BUFFET CAR" appears in large gilt letters across this section. Inside the motif was that everything should be curved; bulk-heads with entrances shaped in Turkish Mosque style led to the ten-seat bar, and tables and chairs were curved; the only ornamentation was a series of decorative

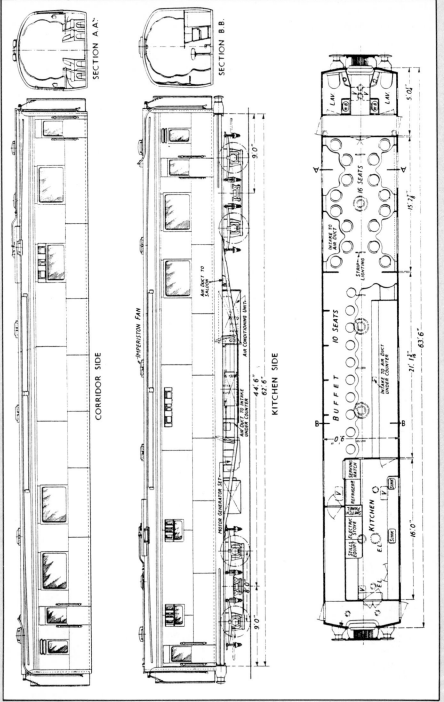

General arrangement of the non-motor bogie buffet cars used on the London–Portsmouth via mid-Sussex express electric trains.

Courtesy, Railway Gazette

plaques designed by Mr G. Kruger Gray on themes of animals and veget-
ables. These cars were staffed by the Pullman Car Co. which had already had
experience of buffet cars converted from Pullmans. The set containing the
buffet car was normally at the rear leaving the London terminus.

The 4 BUF and 4 COR sets worked the line until January 1964 when they
were replaced by 4 CEP and 4 BEP sets. Saturday and Sunday buffet cars
were withdrawn from 14th September, 1963. About 1970 4 CEP sets were
replaced by 4 CIG's; 4 BEP's were replaced by 4 BIG's (buffet units) in 1980.
Local and semi-fast London services are now run by 4 VEP sets, but the 4
VEP's occasionally do a turn on the fast trains.

Visitors to Bognor on 17th August, 1972 may have been forgiven if they
were under the impression that they had boarded the wrong train at Barnham, because the station had been re-named Newhaven Harbour and standing at platform 4, headed by a class '73' diesel, was the Venice–Simplon
Orient Express. Was Bognor aspiring to higher things again? No, not this
time, it was simply a ruse by a film company who were unable to use the real
facilities at Newhaven Harbour.

And lastly with perhaps a taste of things to come at Bognor, a class 155
"Sprinter" has been introduced on the Brighton–Cardiff route, so improving
overall running times for the future.

Saxby and Farmer ground frame serial number 6072, installed at Bognor station in
1901 and still used to release trains from platform three in 1988.   *Author*

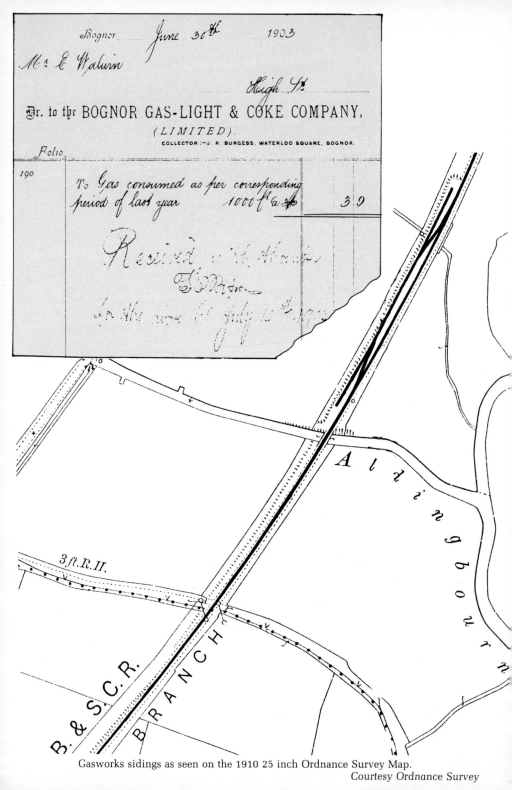

Bognor *June 30th* *1903*

Mr E Walwin

High St.

Dr. to the BOGNOR GAS-LIGHT & COKE COMPANY,
(LIMITED).

COLLECTOR:—J. R. BURGESS, WATERLOO SQUARE, BOGNOR.

Folio

190

To Gas consumed as per corresponding
period of last year   1000 ft @ 3/9   3 | 9

Received with thanks

A l d i n g b o u r n

3 ft. R.H.

B. & S.C.R.

BRANCH

Gasworks sidings as seen on the 1910 25 inch Ordnance Survey Map.

Courtesy Ordnance Survey

Appendix One
Gasworks Siding

In 1903 the Bognor Gas Light and Coke Company applied for Parliamentary permission to build a new "Town Gas" manufactory at a site near Shripney, just north of Bognor. The site was bounded by the Shripney Road to the east, the Aldingbourne Rife to the south and the Bognor branch line to the west. The original plan shows a siding leaving the branch from the Barnham Junction direction at the northern border of the gasworks site and entering the works parallel to the line. After about 20 yards the line splits and the two sidings ran on for approximately 100 yards, still parallel with the branch line, and stopping just short of the Rife. The eastern siding ran into the coal store whilst the other is marked as being a storage siding.

It is not clear when the siding was first used, however it must have been between 1905 and 1910 when the siding is first shown on an Ordnance Survey map, but the 1910 25 in. map shows the line as being built in a totally different way to the original plan. There was only a single siding, with points at either end to allow the locomotive to rejoin the branch line.

The 1911 track doubling brought about a revision of the siding layout, the siding could now only be reached from the Barnham direction. The track doubled soon after the points and, as in the first plan, ran parallel with the branch line; the two sidings joined shortly before the end to allow the engine to run-round its train. Once the coal had been unloaded the wagons were then filled with coke formed during the gas-making process. There were no facilities for the train to cross over to the down line so the wagons had to be reversed on to the up line, and once the points had been re-set, carry on into Bognor on the wrong line. Here the wagons were placed in the fan of coal sidings for unloading and distribution around the town.

In 1969 the production of "town gas" was halted on the introduction of North Sea gas to the town; the gasometers were retained for storage purposes but the gas production buildings were demolished. The land released was sold to LEC Refrigeration, who had built their factory on the northern boundary of the gasworks. The sidings were used to load new refrigerators on to railway wagons for delivery all over the country. LEC continued to use the siding until 1975 when they purchased a fleet of trucks to do their own deliveries and the line fell derelict. The track was finally lifted in 1977 to allow the construction of a new warehouse.

Shripney Road Gasworks, possibly photographed on opening day, 1904.
Gerard Young Collection

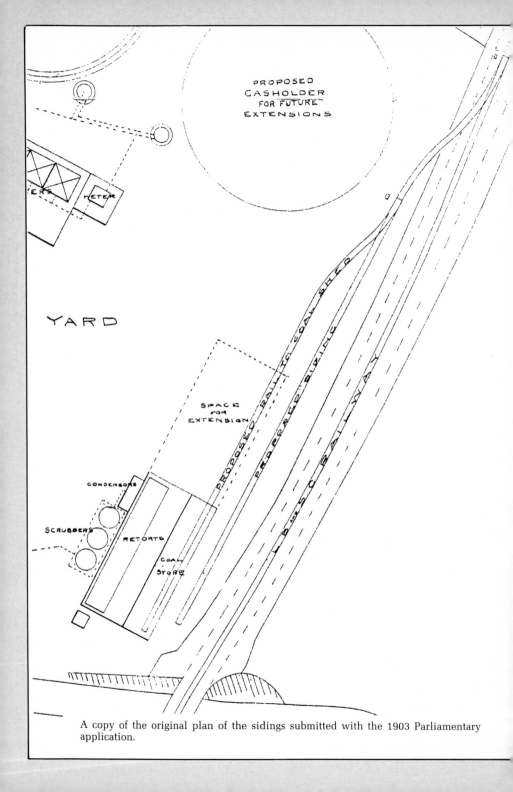

A copy of the original plan of the sidings submitted with the 1903 Parliamentary application.

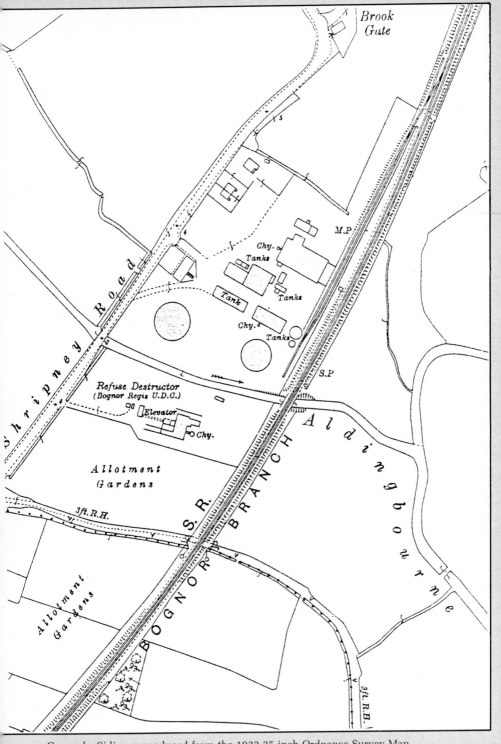

Gasworks Siding, reproduced from the 1932, 25 inch Ordnance Survey Map.
Courtesy Ordnance Survey

'B2x' No. 231 pulls a heavy excursion train out of Bognor in this pre-World War I
view.   *H. Gordon Tidey*

'D1' class No. 239 (ex-*Patcham*) pulls slowly over the ash pit at Bognor locomotive
shed in February 1927. The large number of hose connections were required for
auto-train running.   *R.M. Casserley*

Appendix Two
Headcodes

LB & SCR and Southern Railway until 1934.

White discs or white discs with black crosses were placed on any of six positions on the front of a locomotive, from 1917 only white discs were used.

Barnham Junction−Bognor, Day Ordinary: one white disc on left side of buffer beam.

Barnham Junction−Bognor, Day Special: one white disc on left side of buffer beam and white disc with black cross on top centre of smokebox door.

Victoria/London Bridge−Bognor via Quarry line: square board on top centre of smokebox door (1900−1910).

London Bridge−Portsmouth via local line between Norwood Junction and Bricklayers Arms Junction, Day Ordinary: one white disc on left side of buffer beam.

London Bridge−Portsmouth via local line between Norwood Junction and Bricklayers Arms Junction, Day Special: one white disc on each end of buffer beam.

London Bridge−Portsmouth via main line between Norwood Junction and Bricklayers Arms Junction, Day Ordinary: discs with black cross on top centre of smokebox door, centre and right of buffer beam.

London Bridge−Portsmouth via main line between Norwood Junction and Bricklayers Arms Junction, Day Special: white discs on top centre of smokebox door, centre and right side of buffer beam.

London Bridge−Portsmouth via Redhill and Three Bridges, Day Ordinary: white discs on left and centre of buffer beam.

London Bridge−Portsmouth via Redhill and Three Bridges, Day Special: white discs with black crosses on centre and right of buffer beam and white disc on top centre of smokebox door.

London Bridge−Portsmouth via through lines and Three Bridges, Day Ordinary: two white discs on left of buffer beam and a white disc with black cross on centre of buffer beam.

London Bridge−Portsmouth via through lines and Three Bridges, Day Special: two white discs on left of buffer beam and a white disc with black cross on top centre of smokebox door.

London Bridge−Portsmouth via Peckham Rye, Day Ordinary: one white disc on top centre of smokebox door.

London Bridge−Portsmouth via Peckham Rye, Day Special: one white disc on top centre of smokebox door and one at centre of buffer beam.

Victoria−Portsmouth via Mitcham, Sutton, Epsom, Dorking and Horsham, Day Ordinary: white discs with black cross on top centre of smokebox door and right side of buffer beam.

Victoria−Portsmouth via Mitcham, Sutton, Epsom, Dorking and Horsham, Day Special: white discs with black crosses on top centre of smokebox door and at left and right of buffer beam.

Victoria−Portsmouth via Balham line, Redhill and Three Bridges, Day Ordinary: white discs with black crosses on left and centre of buffer beam.

Victoria−Portsmouth via Balham line, Redhill and Three Bridges, Day Special: white discs with black crosses on left and centre of buffer beam and white disc on right.

Victoria−Portsmouth via Balham line, through line and Three Bridges, Day Ordinary: two white discs with black crosses on left of buffer beam.

Class 'H2' "Atlantic" No. 2425 working hard as it pulls out of Bognor with a London train in March 1937.
L.T. Catchpole

Class 'E3' 0–6–2T No. 462 displays the branch line headcode as it stands over the ash pit at Bognor locomotive shed in April 1926.
R.M. Casserley

Victoria–Portsmouth via Balham line, through line and Three Bridges, Day Special: two white discs with black crosses on left of buffer beam and white disc on centre.

Victoria–Portsmouth via Crystal Palace, West Croydon, Sutton and Horsham, Day Ordinary: one white disc on centre of buffer beam and one white disc with black cross on top centre of smokebox door.

Victoria–Portsmouth via Crystal Palace, West Croydon, Sutton and Horsham, Day Special: one white disc at centre of buffer beam and white discs with black cross top centre of smokebox door and right of buffer beam.

Kensington–Portsmouth via Mitcham Junction, Day Special: white discs on left and centre of buffer beam and top centre of smokebox door.

Brighton–Portsmouth, Day Ordinary: one white disc top centre of smokebox door and white disc with black cross on right side of buffer beam.

Brighton–Portsmouth, Day Special: white disc with black cross on top centre of smokebox door and white disc on each end of the buffer beam.

Horsham–Bognor, Goods Train: white discs on left of smokebox door and centre of buffer beam.

Three Bridges–Portsmouth, Day Special: white disc with black cross on centre of buffer beam and white disc on top centre of smokebox door.

In 1934 the Southern Railway simplified the system so that on normal trains not more than two white discs had to be shown, e.g.:

Bognor–Victoria: one white disc on top centre of smokebox door and one on right side of the smokebox door.

Electric Headcodes 1938–1978

These were numbers carried at first on removable stencils and later on roller blinds on the centre of the driving cab fronts.

1: Barnham–Bognor Regis
3: Arundel–Bognor Regis via Littlehampton
4: Arundel–Bognor Regis, Direct
6: Three Bridges–Bognor Regis
7: Three Bridges/Horsham–Bognor Regis via Littlehampton
10: Bognor Regis–Portsmouth Town
12: Bognor Regis–Portsmouth Harbour
20: Victoria–Portsmouth Harbour via Mitcham Junction
21: London Bridge–Portsmouth Harbour via Mitcham Junction
23: London Bridge–Portsmouth Harbour via Quarry line and Horsham
25: London Bridge–Portsmouth Harbour via Redhill and Horsham
26: Victoria–Portsmouth Harbour via Quarry line and Horsham
28: Victoria–Portsmouth Harbour via Redhill and Horsham
30: Brighton–Portsmouth Harbour via Littlehampton
31: Brighton–Bognor Regis via Littlehampton
40: Victoria–Bognor Regis via Mitcham Junction
41: London Bridge–Bognor Regis via Mitcham Junction
42: Bognor Regis–Victoria via Littlehampton, Horsham and Redhill
43: London Bridge–Bognor Regis via Quarry line and Horsham
45: London Bridge–Bognor Regis via Redhill and Horsham
46: Victoria–Bognor Regis via Quarry line and Horsham
47: London Bridge–Bognor Regis via West Croydon

48:    Victoria–Bognor Regis via Redhill and Horsham
60:    Brighton–Portsmouth Harbour, semi-fast
62:    Brighton–Portsmouth Harbour, slow
64:    Brighton–Bognor Regis
70:    Victoria–Portsmouth Harbour via Mitcham Junction and Littlehampton
71:    London Bridge–Portsmouth Harbour via Mitcham Junction and Littlehampton
73:    London Bridge–Portsmouth Harbour via Quarry line, Horsham and Little-
       hampton
75:    London Bridge–Portsmouth Harbour via Redhill, Horsham and Littlehampton
76:    Victoria–Portsmouth Harbour via Quarry line, Horsham and Littlehampton
78:    Victoria–Portsmouth Harbour via Redhill, Horsham and Littlehampton
90:    Victoria–Bognor Regis via Mitcham Junction and Littlehampton
91:    London Bridge–Bognor Regis via Mitcham Junction and Littlehampton
93:    London Bridge–Bognor Regis via Quarry line, Horsham and Littlehampton
95:    London Bridge–Bognor Regis via Redhill, Horsham and Littlehampton
96:    Victoria–Bognor Regis via Quarry line, Horsham and Littlehampton
98:    Victoria–Bognor Regis via Redhill, Horsham and Littlehampton

Electric Headcodes 1978 onwards

6:     Victoria–Bognor Regis via Quarry line and Horsham
16:    Victoria–Bognor Regis via Redhill
26:    Victoria–Bognor Regis via Quarry line, Horsham and Littlehampton
36:    Victoria–Bognor Regis via Redhill, Horsham and Littlehampton
46:    Victoria–Bognor Regis via Mitcham Junction (until May 1985)
56:    Bognor Regis–Victoria via Littlehampton, Horsham and Redhill

'D3' class 0–4–4T No. 391 at Bognor in February 1927. After the formation of the
Southern Railway, Brighton engines were given a small 'B' over the number, but
later on all ex-LB&SCR locomotives were renumbered by the addition of 2000 to
the old number.   *R.M. Casserley*

Sources

Railway Documents
LB & SCR Special Traffic Notice, No. 18 (4/5/1907).
LB & SCR Special Traffic Notice, No. 20 (18/5/1907).
LB & SCR Special Traffic Notice, No. 25 (22/6/1907).

Maps
Plan and section of the intended Bognor Branch Railway, 1845. (WSRO/ QDP/W94).
Plan and section of the proposed Chichester and Bognor Railway, 1845. (WSRO/QDP/W95).
Plan and section of the proposed Dock and Piers at Bognor, Sussex, 1845. (WSRO/QDP/W100).
Drayton and Bognor Railway, Plan and section, 1846. (WSRO/QDP/W102).
Plan and sections of the proposed Bognor Railway, 1852. (WSRO/QDP/ W108).
Bognor Railway, Session 1857–58. (WSRO/QDP/W118).
Bognor Railway, Session 1860–61. (WSRO/QDP/W132).
Bognor, Chichester and Midhurst Railway, Session 1860–61. (WSRO/QDP/ W133).
Bognor, Chichester and Midhurst Railway, Session 1862–63. (WSRO/QDP/ W139).
LB & SCR Various Powers, Session 1899, plans 32 and 33. (WSRO/QDP/ W210).
Tithe Boundary maps, 1845/6. (WSRO various).

Newspapers
Bognor Observer 1890–1925
Chichester Journal 1860–1864
Chichester Observer 1900–1901
West Sussex Gazette 1860–1920

Printed Sources
Victoria County History, Vol. 2.
Railway Stations, Southern Region, N. Wikeley and J. Middleton, 1971.
A History of Bognor Regis, Young, 1983.
Railways of Mid Sussex, A. Gray, 1975.
The London Brighton and South Coast Railway, J.T. Howard Turner, 1979.
South Coast Railways, Worthing to Chichester, V. Mitchell and K. Smith, 1983.
London, Brighton and South Coast Railway Album, K. Marx and J. Minnis, 1982.
Locomotives of the London Brighton and South Coast Railway, F. Burt, c1903.
Locomotives of the London Brighton and South Coast Railway, D.L. Bradley, 1969.

The Chichester and Midhurst Railway, P. Clark, 1979.
Glimpses of Bognor Regis, S. Endacott, 1985.
A Picture of Bognor Regis, WSCCLAAS, 1976.
Lovett's Guide to Bognor, 1870 and 1875.
Webster and Webb Guide to Bognor, 1892.
Bognor Town Guide, 1900 and 1920.

Periodicals
The Brighton Circular.
The Railway Gazette, Supplement to, 24th June 1938.

Bognor Regis station today; apart from the scalloping having been removed from the canopy barge boards and the addition of a new door into the first window, it is as built in 1902.   *Author*